I0762738

To

From

Date

a place of peace

Devotions to Ease Stress and Enjoy a Calmer Life

DaySpring
LIVE YOUR FAITH

A Place of Peace: Devotions to Ease Stress and Enjoy a Calmer Life

First Edition, February 2026

Published by:

21154 Highway 16 East
Siloam Springs, AR 72761
dayspring.com

Cover Design by: Hannah Brinson

Printed in Vietnam
Prime: U4578
ISBN: 979-8-88603-413-4

Contents

Introduction

Turn from evil and do good; seek peace and pursue it.

PSALM 34:14 NIV

In a world filled with chaos, uncertainty, and trouble, peace can often feel out of reach. We long for rest in the midst of life's storms, yet anxiety, fear, and stress seem to follow us at every turn. But God has not called us to a life of worry—He has called us to a life of peace. Psalm 34:14 reminds us that peace is not something we merely stumble upon; it is something we must actively seek and pursue.

This devotional is an invitation to walk in the peace that God freely offers. Each day, we will explore Scripture, reflect on God's promises, and discover how to cultivate a heart that is steadfast, even in the face of adversity. True peace is not found in perfect circumstances but in the presence of a perfect God. When we anchor ourselves in His truth, we can experience a peace that surpasses understanding, but we must pursue it with the decisions we make each day of our lives.

Whether you are struggling with uncertainty, carrying burdens that feel too heavy, or simply longing for a deeper sense of calm in your daily life, this book is for you. Each entry will share an important message about God's peace and then provide you with specific ways you can pursue that peace in your life. As you embark on this journey, may you find rest in God's love, strength in His promises, and the unwavering peace that only He can provide.

Let's seek peace together—and pursue it with all our hearts!

Christ Jesus, Our Hope

"I am making a way in the wilderness and streams in the wasteland."
ISAIAH 43:19 NIV

Have you ever really listened to how people talk about peace? What about hope? Often these are referred to as a kind of ingredient they can add when they need a little extra oomph in life. Maybe when they're going through a hard time or when they'd really like to see a certain outcome, they might say things like, "This is tough, but at least I have peace about what's going on!" or "I'm trying something new, so I'm just gonna hope for the best!" The hope and peace God offers us is something altogether different from these ideas. They have substance; they sustain us and transform us, even as we wait to see how they will fully bear fruit in our lives. As Romans 5:5 (NLT) reminds us: "This hope will not lead to disappointment. For we know how dearly God loves us, because He has given us the Holy Spirit to fill our hearts with His love." The hope and the peace we find in Christ is not a now-and-then feeling—it's eternal. It's the lens through which we can choose to see everything, every day. We can stake our whole lives on it, and many who've come before us have done just that—and lived beautiful, remarkable lives because of it. Not easy or predictable lives by any means, but unforgettable ones, whose ripple effect will be felt for generations to come. Why did the prophets and the most influential figures in the Bible never give up? Because they lived with that deep, abiding sense of hope. They turned their hearts toward God again and again, even as doubt and discouragement came knocking on their door. They knew that He would always have the last word, and every struggle, challenge, and circumstance they faced would have to fall in line with that truth eventually—and they could rest in the peace those truths brought. Creation is being redeemed—it's headed somewhere beautiful, and no one can derail that eternal plan.

pursue peace

The messages found in this book are for you to read in your own way, at your own pace. They might speak to you differently today than they will tomorrow. Each day, you'll read inspiring words that invite you to experience the peace God gives in a new way. They might speak to something you're struggling with right now, or something you may go through in the future, or even something someone you know is facing in their own life. The thoughts and experiences shared in these devotions are universal—we all know how heavy doubt, disappointment, and discouragement can feel. So, as we walk our own path, we might find ways to help one another find peace along the journey. The more support we can share, the better.

You can also choose how to respond to the thoughts shared in these pages. There will be suggestions for actions that you can take to help bring more of God's peace and hope into your daily life, but you're the one who knows best how to make that happen. And most importantly, God may lead you to take action in unique and surprising ways as you hear Him speak to your heart.

God's Unchanging Nature

Look closely for the fingerprints of God's faithfulness throughout the seasons of your life.

NANCY KAY GRACE

Nature mirrors the image of our Creator in some powerful, inspiring, and breathtaking ways, as the Bible often reminds us. Psalm 19:1–2 (NLT) declares: "The heavens proclaim the glory of God. The skies display His craftsmanship. Day after day they continue to speak: night after night they make Him known." Just think . . . we can walk out the door and look at any part of the earth or sky above and see a reflection of the One who spoke it all into existence. And one of the most encouraging reminders that creation offers us is this: God is dependable. There are certain things about Him that we can count on, no matter what; they've always been true, and they always will be. Think about the patterns you observe in the great outdoors, season after season: At a particular time each year, geese fly south; it's just what they do, by deliberate design. And the lovely green leaves that are slowly dying on our favorite trees as the weather turns cold? We don't worry about losing them forever. Their vibrant replacements are already in the works, due to sprout next spring. How about the tide we see going out each day? We know that it'll find its way back in, just like it has since the beginning of time. Like those patterns in nature, there's a sense of peace that comes with the things we know we can always count on in our lives. We as God's children can rest knowing we're safe in His constant care. Especially when we're navigating life's most uncertain seasons. His unchanging promises can bring us the steadfast peace we need to see us through.

pursue peace

In God's way, in God's time, He is always working for the good of those who love Him. Consider setting aside some time to reflect on the promises below, taken from God's Word. (Feel free to add your own if you wish.) Think about how you've seen each one play out in your life or the life of someone you know. Choose one promise that you find most difficult to hold on to. Ask God to help you experience the truth of that promise in a deeper way in the days to come. You might even write it out and place it somewhere you will see it often. Let it serve as a daily reminder that His truth is infinitely greater than any doubt you may have. And whenever you can, allow nature to remind you of His constant presence and steadfast love—and let this bring you peace.

Promise of Presence:

"Do not fear, for I am with you." Isaiah 41:10 (NIV)

Promise of Guidance:

"He will make your paths straight." Proverbs 3:6 (NIV)

Promise of Comfort:

"He heals the brokenhearted." Psalm 147:3 (NIV)

Promise of Provision:

"My God will meet all your needs." Philippians 4:19 (NIV)

Promise of Salvation:

"By grace you have been saved, through faith." Ephesians 2:8 (NIV)

Today's Tune-Up

Self-care is a divine responsibility.

DANIELLE LAPORTE

Are you one of those people who sees a "check engine" light as simply a nice suggestion? Or when that little indicator flashes on, do you drop everything and call the repair shop without delay? And how about your gas gauge? Will you coast into the station on fumes, or does the needle rarely sink below half-tank?

Many people fall into one of two general categories when it comes to those kinds of things in our lives: proactive and reactive. Some of us just have more laid-back personalities, and others tend to take the bull by the horns. Nothing wrong with either approach, but unfortunately, those of us who fall into the "reactive" camp often have to learn more things the hard way. That's what happens in our spiritual lives too. We may notice some red flags in our attitude or find ourselves feeling like our love tank is low. People are getting on our nerves; we're quicker to judge and slower to give grace; we notice more discouraging thoughts than grateful ones filling our heads. And if we allow that "struggling spirit" light to stay on too long, we can start to feel downright depressed. That's why it's vital for us to maintain our connection with God on the smooth days as well as the rough ones. Instead of waiting until things start going south, we'll surely benefit from checking in from time to time throughout the day, just to feel His presence.

pursue peace

Being proactive to pause for a spiritual tune-up today will make it possible for you to live with more peace and joy tomorrow. Consider asking yourself a few questions about how it's been going lately and journal your answers:

- What's been weighing on my mind and heart, and how can I find more peace about it?
- Are any of my relationships in need of some loving attention?
- How well have I been caring for myself, and are there any healthy steps I need to take?

The Message Bible offers a fresh expression of the familiar fruit-of-the-Spirit verses. Read these words from Galatians 5:22–23 and consider how you're feeling about what is growing in your own life: "But what happens when we live God's way? He brings gifts into our lives, much the same way that fruit appears in an orchard—things like affection for others, exuberance about life, serenity. We develop a willingness to stick with things, a sense of compassion in the heart, and a conviction that a basic holiness permeates things and people. We find ourselves involved in loyal commitments, not needing to force our way in life, able to marshal and direct our energies wisely." Living God's way, including caring for yourself before you need a critical tune-up, is one of the best ways to cultivate His peace in your life!

Happily Ever After

What a wonderful thought it is that some of the best days of our lives haven't even happened yet.
ANNE FRANK

Have you ever met someone who likes to read the last line of a book before they even start it? Yes, it's a thing! While that sounds very strange to some of us, it makes perfect sense to others. Those readers want to know what they're getting themselves into, after all. They're about to invest hours of their life in that story, and they like to make sure the payoff in the end is going to be worth it. Plus, they find the whole experience to be less stressful and more fulfilling when they already know whether the villain is going to get away with something, or if those two lovebirds are going to find their way back to each other.

So what does this have to do with our spiritual journeys? Well, whether we like spoilers or not, God has already told us where our story is headed . . . somewhere beyond our wildest dreams. And Jesus promises us in Revelation that He is going to take us there: "I am coming soon" (Revelation 22:12 ESV). No matter what happens between this breath and the last one we take, we can depend on that promise to be our happily-ever-after . . . and it's no fantasy. As we've all discovered, this story we're living is very real, and not at all easy, but so worth it. We can live with hopeful hearts from our first page to our final one on this earth, holding fast to Jesus's promise: "When everything is ready, I will come and get you, so that you will always be with Me where I am" (John 14:3 NLT).

pursue peace

Imagine you've discovered someone who has never heard of Jesus, never read even one of God's promises—someone who looks around at the world today and thinks this is as good as it gets. They believe that when the last chapter of their life on earth is written, that's the end of the story. Period. Now, imagine that you get to be the one to tell them the Good News—that there's Someone who created them and loves them so much that He not only made a way for them to live with joy and peace in this life, but He has also prepared a place for them that's beyond what they could ever imagine. Find a pen and some paper and write that person a letter. Tell them whatever you want to about your life—maybe share what it was like before you met Jesus or heard of God's love. Maybe tell them why you live with peace each day, even when you're going through tough times. Now try reading those words out loud. You'll be reminded in a new way that the peace you have in your life because of Jesus is very real, and that no matter what you're facing today, your story does have a happily-ever-after. You've been headed toward it ever since the day God called you to Himself. And that's a page that is definitely worth reading.

Life Beyond Limits

God can do anything, you know—far more than you could ever imagine or guess or request in your wildest dreams!
EPHESIANS 3:20 THE MESSAGE

What do you think of when you hear the word *limitless*? Maybe the vast, deep blue ocean or an endless, star-filled sky? It can be hard for our minds to hold the thought of infinite anything when we're so used to inhabiting these limited bodies of ours. We live in a world of boundaries and measurements; it's how we humans coexist and make sense of things on this marvelous planet we call home. We live with limits here, and when it comes to resources, we've discovered that there's only so much of this or that thing to go around—so when it's gone, it's gone! It can be scary when there's a shortage of something, when it seems like everyone's scrambling to get whatever they need, however they can, when the world seems less like a kindergarten classroom (Everyone, take turns and share!) and more like a battle zone (survival of the fittest!). Our trust that God will provide all we need can waver, and our mindset can go from abundance to scarcity pretty quickly. As soon as we take our eyes off our Provider and focus more on the provision, things start to head south, because the provision may be limited, but the Provider is limitless. And He designed us in such a way that our satisfaction can only be found in Him. No amount of anything can ever replace that truth. So when we catch ourselves feeling the familiar fear of "not enough" creep up, it's a great reminder to take our eyes once again off the world around us and find hope in the One whose Spirit lives within us.

pursue peace

Next time you notice that worry or uncertainty has started clouding your days, consider reading Luke 12:22–34 (aka, the "stop overthinking" verses). As you do so, you might use your imagination to envision yourself sitting with Jesus while He was speaking those words on earth. See Him smile at you reassuringly as He gestures toward the birds of the air and the flowers in the field, demonstrating how beautifully the natural world reflects a worry-free existence. While we are designed to do good and meaningful work and provide for our families, in the midst of it all, we have a choice: We can hold all we possess today with a tight fist as we fret about getting more tomorrow, or we can relax more and more into the care of our Maker, being grateful for what we have and trusting that He will provide everything we need when we need it. The truth is, no one will ever have "enough" to feel completely safe or satisfied in this lifetime. We can experience seasons of greater comfort and prosperity, but it isn't helpful to allow our peace to depend on those times, because they will eventually slip away. That's just the nature of things. Our God, however, is here for the long haul. He has an endless supply of what we need to thrive each day, and He's not going anywhere. The more we're able to trust in that, the more freedom and joy we'll live with every day.

PAUSE FOR PRAYER

Heavenly Father,

I come before You with a heart burdened by the turmoil of this world. Lord, You are the Prince of Peace, the One who calms the storms and brings order to chaos. I ask for Your divine peace to fill my heart and my home today. Grant me the courage to be an instrument of Your peace, to sow love where there is hatred and to foster understanding where there is division. Help me to see other people through Your eyes, with compassion and grace.

Teach me to be a peacemaker in my words and actions, to forgive as You have forgiven me, and to seek reconciliation wherever there is discord. May Your peace, which surpasses all understanding, guard my heart and my mind in Christ Jesus. I place my trust in You, Lord, knowing that You are able to bring a peace that endures. May I trust in You more each day, placing all of my cares upon You.

In Jesus's name, amen.

More Than Words

We don't need perfect words; we just need open hearts.

ANONYMOUS

Raise your hand if you've ever been at a loss for words when trying to comfort or encourage someone who was going through a hard time. At some point, most of us have found our tongues tied, even though our hearts were wide open, just wishing we knew how to say what someone needed to hear. We can do our very best to try to put ourselves into the shoes of another, but at the end of the day, they are the only ones who are walking that path, and no one else knows exactly how it feels.

What matters most in these situations isn't that we find the perfect words but that we simply offer ourselves as vessels of God's love. Imperfect as we are, we show up and share whatever we can, trusting that He will always use our best intentions for good.

And here's an important note for those of us who are going through hard times ourselves: when we are on the *receiving* end of that support, let us remember that others are doing the best *they* can to lift us up. They want us to know we're not alone; they want us to feel God's peace amid our struggles; they want to shine a light of hope so we can see that those darker times won't last forever. And if they clam up or stumble over their words, if they say something that feels like sandpaper even though they were going for silk, let's remember where their hearts are and sense God's loving presence even in their effort.

Pursue Peace

Words can be tricky, even when we use them with the best intentions. That's a great thing to be aware of when it comes to supporting each other through tough times. Consider the following thoughts as you make those future connections:

Before reaching out to lift someone up, take a moment to ask for God's timing and direction. Just a simple prayer can make a big difference: *Lord, please give me the words and actions this person needs most, right when they are needed.*

If you're not sure what to say or do, be honest. Let the person know that you don't have the words, but you want to show up for them however they need. Offer your presence. Sitting silently with someone can bring more peace and strength than we may ever realize. God can do a lot in a quiet space with an open heart. As Paul reminds us, "In the same way, the Spirit helps us in our weakness. We do not know what we ought to pray for, but the Spirit Himself intercedes for us" (Romans 8:26 NIV).

Let's give thanks to a loving Father who never leaves us alone in our discouraging times. He will always send light in the darkness, and how beautiful it is that we get to be the messengers who carry it to one another.

Rising Higher

"Do not worry about tomorrow, for tomorrow will worry about itself."

MATTHEW 6:34 NIV

Disappointment and *discouragement*. Just the sound of those two words is enough to make us cringe. And when they come knocking on the doors of our hearts? Well, most of us would rather pretend we're not home . . . and who could blame us? We all go through those times of feeling defeated in life, and they can't end soon enough. Maybe it happens when we fall short of those high expectations we've set for ourselves, or when we wonder if that dream of ours will ever get off the ground, or when we're frustrated that we've missed the mark yet again, or we just can't figure out the key to success in some area we're passionate about. We feel a heaviness in our days, our hope flame flickers, and sometimes we wonder if things will ever change for the better. That's when we need to remind ourselves that what we see as a "mistake" or a "failure," God sees very differently. It's not that He *wants* us to miss that mark, of course, but He already knows all the ways He's going to use it for our good and His glory. Our job is to trust Him in that—especially in our most defeated moments. We always have the choice: We can use our energy to beat ourselves up, overthink every misstep we made, sink into shame, or blame someone else. Or we can redirect that energy toward trusting the One who has already set new opportunities in motion—the One who's working behind the scenes to grow us through our struggles and to grace us with greater compassion for ourselves and others.

Pursue Peace

A life surrendered to God is always moving in a hopeful direction, even when we can't feel it! Try this: Find some paper and make a single dot on it. Then, from that dot, draw a circle that begins and ends in the same spot. Trace the circle over and over again, noticing how you keep coming back to that original dot. It's impossible not to, right? Now, beside it, draw a spiral, allowing your pencil to circle around and around as it gradually climbs higher and higher. Trace that spiral a few times, just like you did the circle, but notice that you never come back to the same exact spot. Your pencil may travel back around, but it is always moving higher. When we deal with repeated disappointment or discouragement in our lives, it can feel like that circle—going around and around and just not getting anywhere. But when we begin to see our journey the way God does, we understand that even if we experience familiar setbacks, we are always rising higher—because He's using every little thing for our good. With God, there is no dead end, no endless cycle of defeat, no meaningless running on a hamster wheel of life. Once we put our trust in Him, there's only one direction for us to head, and that's the road of hope and peace.

Counting Down

Do what you can, with what you've got, where you are.

THEODORE ROOSEVELT

If you've ever had school kids in your home (or remember being one), you might be familiar with the following words, likely uttered in dramatic fashion: *When will I ever need math in my real life?!* Well, besides those engineers, architects, and astronomers who surely have detailed answers to that question, the rest of us can at least agree on this simple mathematical life lesson: Dealing with big numbers takes much more work than dealing with small ones. For instance, when we look at the headlines in our daily lives and see the devastation of a natural disaster or a large population of people in need, it can feel really overwhelming to us. Our hearts may break as we watch so many of our fellow human beings struggle; our heads may spin as we wonder what we could possibly do to help. But remember, we're looking at big numbers, which always feel like more than we can handle. So, let's start small instead. We can't do something for everyone, but we can always do something for *someone*. We can take that headline about one million people and choose to focus on just one. How that happens will be between us and our Maker. But when we take that prayerful step to offer our resources and abilities back to the One who provided them in the first place, He will gladly use what we have to help us make a difference. And even if that difference is for just one person, it's enough—because every single one of us has infinite worth in God's eyes.

Pursue Peace

You may have heard the story about an old man standing on a beach after a storm that's just caused thousands of starfish to be washed up and stranded on the shore. The man catches sight of a young boy walking toward him, stooping over every few steps to reach down for one of those stranded creatures and throw it back into the water so it can live. The man asks the boy why he's bothering to do that when there were so many. "What does it matter?" he says. "There are thousands. You can't really make that much of a difference." The boy lifts the starfish he's holding and says, "But it matters to this one," as he tosses it back into the sea.

God values each of us infinitely, and even when the numbers seem overwhelming, He calls us to reach out, one by one, to touch the lives of our fellow humans. Consider spending some time in prayer to ask God how you might bless someone with the unique abilities and resources He's given you. Maybe an answer will be clear right away, or perhaps it'll be revealed in the coming days. Regardless, there's one thing you can always count on: every soul on this earth matters infinitely to Him, and that includes yours.

Together We Shine

You are all children of the light and children of the day.

I THESSALONIANS 5:5 NIV

A popular children's toy in the 1980s involved poking tiny, translucent pegs, one by one, into patterns on black paper. Each peg had an assigned spot, and once they were all added together, a light was flipped on behind the paper to illuminate the colorful image that had been created by the pegs. Kids loved to take their creations into extra-dark rooms because that's when they could really see the luminous picture they had created.

If you think about it, we are like those single pegs before they come together to make a picture—each of us going about our daily lives, uniquely created human beings sharing this great big planet with nearly eight billion others. As we face life's inevitable changes and challenges along the way, we can sometimes feel very alone in our struggles. But it doesn't take long—whether it be a conversation we overhear, a prayer request from a friend, or someone's brutally honest social media post—to realize that everyone is facing *something* that they're hoping to make it through. But not everyone has the hope we have in Christ. When we put our hope in Him, our lives are illuminated in a way that they've never been before. And as others who know Him do the same, their lights shine, too, and God gathers us to create a beautiful picture for the world to see.

Pursue Peace

Galatians 3:26 (NLT) reminds us: "For you are all children of God through faith in Christ Jesus." We're family, in spirit. That means, of course, we are individuals with our own struggles and strengths, but we will always share the love of one Father. While there will be different reasons for each of us to seek guidance and reassurance throughout our lives, there will always be one infinite Source for us to draw from: "The One who is the true light, who gives light to everyone" (John 1:9 NLT). How about you today? When you struggle with something, do you tend to do it alone, or are you able to reach out for support on the journey? And when someone else is walking through a tough time, do you offer your presence and loving attention? Sometimes we don't know what to do—whether it be for ourselves or others—and it leaves us feeling a little (or a lot) in the dark. But the moment our hearts whisper, "Help," our God is there, ready to show us the way. Pay attention to the people in your life and the source of their peace. Draw near to the ones who seek the light of Christ in the dark. You can help each other find your way together as you follow Him.

Making Meaning

Symbols are the language of something invisible spoken in the visible world.

GERTRUD VON LE FORT

People have used symbols to make meaningful connections for centuries. Whether they represent a shared language or a form of self-expression, symbols are a quick way to get a message across, and these days, we're all for that because . . . *the quicker the better!* We communicate without words more than we may realize. We're surrounded by accessories, brand logos, computer apps, and let's not forget that ever-growing world of emojis! And while each of those symbols is created with a specific purpose in mind, they will likely represent something different for each of us as we view them through the lens of our belief systems, our life experiences, and our unique perspectives.

Even the sacred symbol of the cross means different things to different followers of Jesus. Of course, it is the shared symbol of our faith in Him, but it can also reflect even more about our personal spiritual journeys. For instance, one person might glance at a cross and immediately be reminded of the day they gave their heart to Him; another might feel gratitude for the specific things He's freed them from; another might feel the sense of belonging they value in being part of God's family; and of course, for many of us, the cross is a powerful symbol of the hope that sustains us through every day of our lives.

Pursue Peace

Think about the symbols you're surrounded by in your life. Which ones mean the most to you? It doesn't have to be something you can hold in your hand either. For some of us, a certain kind of bird reminds us of a loved one; a tree might make us think of strength and flexibility; the moon glowing with the sun's light symbolizes the way we shine with God's love. The possibilities are endless. How about you? What stories do you carry in your heart about the images you see around you? Focus specifically on peace for a moment. What in your surroundings represents peace to you? It may take some exploration, or perhaps there's something you can think of that is already part of your story. But whatever you choose, ask God to remind you of the symbols that tell *your* story from time to time. It can be one of those sweet and simple ways your heart connects with His in your daily life. You may even wish to keep a little picture of your favorite symbols on your phone or mirror or somewhere you'll pass by often. Sometimes the things that help sustain us on the journey seem pretty simple, but their purpose in inspiring us to connect with our Maker is immense.

PAUSE FOR PRAYER

Dear Jesus,

In a world often filled with uncertainty and unrest, I turn to You, my Source of perfect peace. You are the Creator of harmony, the One who brings stillness to my anxious heart and calm to every storm I face.

Lord, I ask for Your peace to cover me like a gentle rain, refreshing my spirit and renewing my hope. Fill my heart with Your presence, reminding me that in You, I can find shelter and strength. May Your peace take root in my soul, pushing out fear, anger, and despair.

I pray for peace in my relationships—help me to listen with humility, to speak with kindness, and to love with patience. I ask for peace in my community—teach me to bridge divides, to work for justice, and to care for others as You care for me. And Lord, I plead for peace in my world—bring an end to conflicts, soften hardened hearts, and guide all people toward reconciliation.

Lord, let Your peace reign in my life, a reflection of Your Kingdom here on earth. I trust in Your goodness and rest in the promise of Your unending love.

In Jesus's name, amen.

Rise and Shine

When you arise in the morning, think of what a precious privilege it is to be alive, to breathe, to think, to enjoy, to love.

MARCUS AURELIUS

Jesus reminds us often that what's going on in our hearts is the most important thing of all. No matter what we might face in a day, no matter who may challenge or judge us, no matter how much validation we feel from the world outside . . . nothing matters more than what's happening within. That's why it makes such a difference to begin each day by turning our attention to our heart center—that place where God is present at any moment to connect with us. As we meet Him there in the silence of our being (before rushing into all our doing), we take our first step onto a more peaceful path for the day because the state of our hearts will always determine the way we experience the world. The Bible reminds us: "Keep vigilant watch over your heart; that's where life starts" (Proverbs 4:23 The Message).

When we find ourselves feeling down, it's natural for most of us to look around for what may be causing it: relationship clashes, stressful work situations, health issues, global unrest. And while these things are difficult for all of us, the true source of discouragement lies within . . . in our own hearts. The way we respond to what happens in our lives is always within our power, even if we forget that sometimes. It is a freedom given to us by our Maker, and He's there to remind us of that wonderful gift as often as we need.

Pursue Peace

Mornings can be challenging for a lot of us. Before our eyes even flutter open, we may already feel the demands of the day trying to shake us out of bed and nudge us toward that ever-present to-do list. Finding a few moments to set our hearts on a more peaceful path can make a really big difference.

Here are a few questions you can ask yourself at the start of the day (or just every once in a while) to help you tune in to your heart and lean into your Maker:

- How do I feel about this day?
- Are there any "clouds" hanging over my head, and if so, why?
- What is happening in my heart that may be causing this heaviness?
- What are a few ways I can free myself to feel differently today?

At the start of each day, ask the Lord to help you become more aware of what's happening within you; allow Him to reveal any negative thoughts or attitudes you need to let go of. Envision yourself moving through the day with a sense of hope and gratitude. And if outward circumstances threaten to shake things up, just take a deep breath and return to your heart center where you'll always find God's Spirit offering you His peace.

Shaking It Up

Be patient. The best things happen unexpectedly.
ANONYMOUS

Is there anyone in your life whose timeline has looked very different than what's often considered "normal" or expected in our culture? For instance, maybe they were just beginning their dream job when others their age were retiring; or when their peers were settling down to start families, they were just beginning to explore the world; or perhaps they suddenly discovered an ability they had that changed the course of their life. There are so many examples of people who've taken unexpected detours and achieved unlikely goals, it's a wonder we limit anyone with our expectations. We tend to gravitate toward what's familiar in life because it feels safer. So, when people surprise us by pushing boundaries and choosing unexpected paths, it can be a wonderful wake-up call. They remind us that nothing is set in stone—that every day brings possibilities we could never have predicted. If we want to live the most purposeful and fulfilling lives imaginable, then we have to stop limiting ourselves to business as usual. Should we assume that just because most of our friends went to college twenty years ago, it's probably not going to happen for us? Or if we're hoping to find a partner in life and it doesn't seem to be working out, that we've likely missed the boat? Or how about that thing we just *know* we've been called to do, but none of the pieces are coming together . . . *what's up with that?* Should we just give up? Our tiny human expectations pale in comparison to the limitless possibilities God holds for our lives. The more we let go of the timelines we cling to, the more space we have for Him to work.

Pursue Peace

When we find ourselves feeling "stuck" or we have that "never-gonna-happen" feeling weighing us down, we can remember that *no one knows* like God knows. He can take what looks like a dead end to us and turn it into a new beginning in an instant. He can take our average expectations and blow them clean out of the water with something we never even dreamed of. Centuries ago, a man named Job poured every ounce of his faith into God, trusting Him to show up at a time of deep uncertainty: "I know that You can do all things; no purpose of Yours can be thwarted" (Job 42:2 NIV). He goes on to acknowledge that human tendency we all have: "Surely I spoke of things I did not understand, things too wonderful for me to know" (Job 42:3 NIV). And that's the heart of the matter for all of us: There are things ahead on our journeys too wonderful for us to know. There are things we think we *want* that God will replace with what He knows we *need* in order to experience the most fulfilling lives imaginable. Our job is to let go (again and again) and trust His process.

Living Hope

Faith goes up the stairs that love has built and looks out the windows which hope has opened.
CHARLES SPURGEON

Have you ever heard the theory that the five closest people in your life have the greatest effect on your well-being? Supposedly, it's those few people we most commonly interact with who have the strongest influence on our behavior and our attitudes—which makes sense. Of course, there are many factors that play into how we show up in our lives (most significantly, our relationship with God), but it's hard to deny that we are influenced, at least a little, by those we surround ourselves with. We are relational beings, after all, and the people with whom we have significant connections are going to affect us in one way or another.

Think about those you spend the most time around (not counting toddlers and teens). Whom do you interact with regularly, and how does it make you feel to be in their presence? Can you name one or more truly positive people in your life—people who choose to look at the bright side and inspire you to do the same? It's nearly impossible to spend time around an uplifting person without feeling a little lighter, a little more hopeful. It's as if these people have an essence of hope living within them, like a tune without words. Those people in our lives who carry that upbeat tune are true blessings, and we, in turn, have the opportunity to pass that gift along to others.

Pursue Peace

In Paul's Spirit-filled pep talk to the Thessalonians, he reminds them, "Rejoice always, pray continually, give thanks in all circumstances" (I Thessalonians 5:16–18 NIV). As we allow praise, prayer, and gratitude to become more evident in our lives over time, it will affect not only us but also the people around us. A truly joyful heart cannot help but spill over into others, and by God's design, that creates a ripple effect that reaches further than we may ever know. Here's a little tune-up we can give our hearts anytime, anywhere, and it only takes a few moments. We can ask ourselves these three questions, based on Paul's words:

- What's one reason I have to rejoice in God today?
- Whom or what can I lift up in prayer in this moment?
- What's one new thing I am thankful for?

It's that simple. Praise. Pray. Give thanks. And just like every other habit we form, when we do it consistently, we'll find that it starts to shape us in new ways. As we begin to carry a soul-deep sense of hope, we will naturally fulfill the call to "encourage one another and build each other up" (I Thessalonians 5:11 NIV), not just because it's something we *do* all the time but because it's who we *are*.

The View from Above

It's not what you look at that matters. It's what you see.

HENRY DAVID THOREAU

At some point in life, many of us—regardless of how strong our faith is, how much we've grown, or how successful our endeavors have been—still ask ourselves things like: *Is my life really going anywhere? Does it mean anything? What kind of lasting difference have I made in the world?* Even those who know that our ultimate significance lies in the fact that we are God's beloved children, regardless of what we've accomplished, we still have that desire to know not just *that* we matter . . . but *how* we matter. We look at the string of days behind us and try to see how they might reveal a life well-lived. And as we do so, we're likely to find some great things—some wonderful accomplishments and right decisions and life-giving relationships. But we may also find some moments we're not so proud of—some unfinished business, hurtful interactions, and frankly, a few paths we just wish we hadn't taken. That's when it is helpful to zoom out a bit and see the bigger picture. Think of looking out the window of an airplane. The higher you get, the more you see how everything is connected—tiny squares of land interwoven by threads of winding roads. It's a patchwork quilt of farms and cities, rivers and mountains, coexisting meaningfully with one another. And if you could take out one of those patches, it would be like a missing puzzle piece, affecting everything around it. That's exactly how it is with our lives: every part has significance as the past, present, and future are woven together into God's beautiful purpose for us.

Pursue Peace

When we're feeling discouraged about our purpose in life, drawing closer to our heavenly Father can help us see things in a clearer, more meaningful way. Think about it like this: Say you have a friend standing several feet away from you with her phone held up, ready to snap a picture of something that you can't quite see. You're curious about what she's viewing through that lens, but you know that the only way to see what she's seeing is to move closer to her. That's an illustration of how God invites us to lean in to Him as we look at our own lives. If we want to get a better idea of how He sees things, we can ask Him for help with our perspective. Of course, that doesn't mean we'll have answers to all the "whys" or suddenly comprehend the intricate web of connections we're involved in, but it *does* mean that we will have more peace about how it's all coming together for our highest good. Spend some time in prayer asking if there's anything God has for you to see about any past situations, your current circumstances, or any future fears. Ask Him, most of all, to fill you with a sense of reassurance that He is weaving it all together for your good.

Feeling the Burn

If we don't change, we don't grow. If we don't grow, we aren't really living.

GAIL SHEEHY

Do you have any candles around your house that have never been lit? Maybe they're fancy-looking and ornate or they match your décor perfectly, and you don't want to burn them down . . . so you just leave them out to look pretty. It's a funny thing about candles; when they're doing what they're made to do, they don't keep that lovely façade for long. They burn and soften and change shape, disappearing slowly, sometimes ending in a lumpy heap.

If you think about it, we humans often see ourselves like those untouched candles. We have this expectation that our lives aren't supposed to get messy or change form. Things aren't supposed to get uncomfortable or hurt, and when they do, there's *surely* something wrong with us. The truth is, our Maker didn't create us to sit on a shelf looking pretty, collecting dust. He knew from the beginning of time that we would face challenges and that our lives would change form many times. He knew that as we surrendered our old lives in order to become more and more like Christ, those "selves" we tried to create without Him would gradually disappear in order for something real and eternal to take shape in us. This is why, when we're feeling the "burn" of the most difficult things, we must remind ourselves that it all has purpose. God uses it all for good, and not one drop of it will be wasted.

Pursue Peace

Spend some time in prayer and reflection, thinking back to some of the hardest seasons in your life. Now ask God to remind you of the ways He worked in those situations: maybe through the support of someone who showed up for you or a resource that brought you some comfort or even a healthy distraction to help you through a rough patch. Even if you can't think of one silver lining, you can simply be grateful that you survived whatever it was and that you know He had a hand in it.

Whatever you are going through today, God stands ready to provide the comfort and reassurance you need. Consider reading the stories of His people throughout history—Moses, Joseph, David, and many others—who had to trust that their heavenly Father had allowed their challenges for reasons that they could not yet understand. But in that trust, they found freedom, right in the middle of the mess of life . . . and we can too. Just remember, you are never alone when you're feeling the "burn." We are all learning to let go of our idea of what our lives are supposed to look like so that our Maker can shape us into the beautiful creations He already sees when He looks at us today.

PAUSE FOR PRAYER

Loving Father,

I come to You with a heart that longs for peace—peace that only You can provide. Life can feel overwhelming, with its demands, uncertainties, and struggles. But I know that in Your presence, there is rest for my soul and calm for my spirit.

Lord, I ask for Your peace to fill every corner of my life. Quiet the noise within me, the worries that steal my joy, and the fears that keep me from trusting fully in You. Help me to surrender my burdens to You, knowing that You care for me and will never leave me.

Teach me to rest in Your promises and to find strength in Your Word. Remind me that You are in control, even when life feels chaotic. Guide my thoughts and actions that I may reflect Your peace to those around me.

Lord, let Your peace guard my heart and mind, anchoring me in Your love. Help me to walk in harmony with You, trusting You in all things.

In Jesus's name I pray. Amen.

Thinking Bigger

Never be limited by other people's limited imaginations.

DR. MAE JEMISON

In the 1500s, the term *pigeonhole* was first used to describe a tiny place within a large coop of birds where pigeons were put to rest. Today, of course, we use that term to describe what happens when people think "small" about one another—when we make very narrow assumptions about each other without first considering all the qualities or characteristics someone might possess. Unfortunately, this happens more than we realize. It's not that we intentionally *try* to underestimate the potential or worth of another person; in fact, we may not be conscious of it. But it's been happening with humans, in one way or another, since the beginning of time.

It shouldn't surprise any of us to know that Jesus was not a "pigeonholer" in any way. He looked at the high and mighty Pharisee the same way He looked at the down-and-out person on the street. He did not allow their culture, class, status, or any other category that the world used to define them, to limit His belief in their potential. He was always inviting people into freedom with His words, challenging them to see that—as God's creations—they were more than they ever realized. And of course, the same is true for us today. When we keep our minds and hearts open for one another, we follow in His footsteps. And when *we're* the ones who feel undervalued or underestimated, we need to remember that our worth is determined by God alone . . . and that worth is infinite.

Pursue Peace

Here are two questions we can ask ourselves to live free of those limiting beliefs:

How do I tend to think small about others—even unintentionally?

Consider how you perceive your fellow humans—not only those with whom you share close relationships but the people "out there" in the world. Are there certain people you've formed opinions or made judgments about? And can you see how those limitations really are unnecessary and can even be hurtful? Ask God to help you hold more space and grace for other human beings, acknowledging that He is the only One who truly knows each of us inside and out.

How does it affect me when others think small about me?

There will always be people in your life who have opinions about what kind of person you are and what you're capable of. This is hard to hear for many of us because we just wish others would mind their own business! We can instead root ourselves more strongly than ever in God's truth about who we are because, in the end, that's the only truth that makes a difference! Don't shrink to fit anyone's narrow assumptions about you; always see yourself growing in Christ. He is the One who determines the possibilities for your life, and no human can come close to understanding you the way He can.

Feeling It All

You cannot protect yourself from sadness
without protecting yourself from happiness.
JONATHAN SAFRAN FOER

Grief is something many of us don't like to talk about, and it's *definitely* something we wish we didn't have to experience. We all know that it doesn't only show up when someone we love dies; it's a natural process we go through for many reasons in our lives: the necessary end of a friendship; letting go of our attachment to something we've held dear; having to move away and leave a place behind where we've made so many memories. They may be different, but there is one hopeful thing they all share in common: *The grief we allow ourselves to feel today will become fertile ground for joy tomorrow.* That can be hard to believe while we're in the midst of it, but when we look back one day, we will surely see how true it is. As we feel the sadness of loss, we also honor and deeply appreciate those gifts we were given, no matter how long we were able to enjoy them. As we draw close to God and witness His tender heart toward us, we become vessels of compassion for ourselves and for others.

Jesus knew what it was to grieve—not only during that oft-quoted time when He wept at the loss of His friend Lazarus but also through all the "letting gos" that He surely had to do as a human on this earth. We can find hope and take comfort in the fact that He knows exactly how to lead us through our own times of loss.

Pursue Peace

Here's an experiment that can illustrate how important it is for us to feel the things we need to feel. Wherever you are right now, take a deep breath and hold it in as long as you can. While you're holding that breath, though, feel what happens in your body. You'll probably tense up a bit; your mind will start wondering when you're going to feel some relief; you may even get a little anxious. That's what can happen on a heart level when we try to stuff down our sadness for too long. We may not even realize it, but those unexpressed feelings can cause a lot of unrest within us. Now, take some long, slow, deep breaths. Feel how they bring a sense of calm throughout your body. This is what can happen when we let our feelings flow. Since we're often unaware of the extra weight we sometimes carry in our hearts, it's good to ask God once in a while to reveal anything we might need to let go of in order to make room for more peace. When we discover we're carrying something we don't want to carry anymore and we're ready to experience greater freedom within, we can always count on a loving Father who stands ready to take our hand and walk us through it.

Deep Time

All we have to decide is what to do with the time that is given us.

J.R.R. TOLKIEN

Many of us grew up hearing sayings like "a watched clock never ticks" or "a watched pot never boils," when we were hyperfocused on something we just *could not wait one more minute for!* It's a tendency many of us share: we set these expectations, and until they're met (preferably sooner than later), we won't be truly happy and satisfied. We'll just be . . . *waiting*. There are so many other things going on around us, but those things don't matter so much because they're not what we've been hoping for. And as we set our laser focus on what we want, as we tap our feet with impatience, anticipating that *ding!* or delivery or reward or whatever else our instantly gratified world has convinced us we need right now . . . we often miss something much more important. We miss what God has for us in this moment, right here.

Let's be clear though: there's nothing wrong with anticipation. It's all part of the journey! God created us with the capacity for hope, and how wonderful that we get to experience that inner knowing that good things are on their way in our lives. But as we look forward to those things, let us never forget where our feet are *right now*. That is what will bring us true peace. And we will enjoy the whole experience of life so much more if we leave the timing to God and turn our awareness toward *what is* . . . here and now.

Pursue Peace

Second Peter 3:8 (NIV) offers us this reminder about the time outside of time where God dwells: “Do not forget this one thing, dear friends: With the Lord a day is like a thousand years, and a thousand years are like a day.” The Bible reminds us often that our earthly ways of measuring things can be very different from God’s. We may be counting the minutes or days until some kind of “arrival,” but our Creator offers us a much fuller, more immediate life experience that isn’t dependent on the ticking hands of a clock. He invites us to live fully and contentedly, right where we are, even as we wait for future things. Here’s a challenge: start paying attention to what’s pulling you out of the present. Whether it’s checking your phone or fantasizing about how wonderful life will be *as soon as* . . . (fill in the blank), when you notice that you’re in your head, missing what’s right in front of you, take a deep breath, return to the moment with grateful awareness, and say, “Thank You, Lord, for *what is*, right now.” Even if it only happens once a day, over time this simple practice can help you become more aware of the blessings that presently surround you, even as you anticipate all the good the future can bring.

Dear Me

Talk to yourself like you would to someone you love.

BRENÉ BROWN

When we were kids, we did a lot of waiting for someone bigger to help us with those things we weren't grown enough to do—things like reaching high shelves, driving us to baseball games, or making us our favorite grilled cheese. But more significantly, we often looked to those grown-ups to tell us they were proud of what we did, to encourage us when we were down and out, to check under the bed for monsters and reassure us that there were none. If we had the blessing of loving caregivers in our lives, we knew there was someone we could count on to say the words we most needed to hear. Fast-forward to adulthood, and here we are, needing to hear some of those same things: *It's going to be okay. You're safe. You're loved. You matter. You're not alone.* And it's wonderful when we have family, friends, church communities, and other folks in our lives who can remind us of those truths.

But here's the kicker: there's no guarantee that the words of encouragement, affirmation, or reassurance that we're waiting for will come from outside of us. If we wait until they do, we put our sense of well-being into the hands of someone else. And that's not how we were designed to live our best lives. God has given us the wonderful ability to speak to our own hearts—to tell ourselves the truth we need to hear in any situation and to allow it to bring us the peace that is always available to us in Him.

Pursue Peace

What do you need to hear right now in your life? How about when you first wake up in the morning? Or when you feel beat down? Do you need peace? A reminder that you're enough, in this moment, exactly as you are? Just pretend for today that nothing you need to hear will come from outside yourself. Any words your heart longs to receive are up to *you* to provide. And you're going to do it (if you choose to participate) in a letter to yourself. Write "Dear Me" at the top of your journal page, paper, or computer screen. Take a deep breath, close your eyes, and ask yourself what words you most need to hear right now. Be aware of God's loving presence with you and ask Him to show you how you may be waiting for someone else to validate you or encourage you or just let you know it's all going to be okay. You might then read what you write out loud to yourself and let that wonderful truth sink in. In the days ahead, you might become even more aware of the ways you wait for things to come from outside yourself. When you notice that happening, gently remind yourself that God has already provided all you need within.

Clean Living

The best way to find out what we really need is to get rid of what we don't.

MARIE KONDO

Spring cleaning is a practice many of us are familiar with. Maybe it's something our grandparents or parents did, or we might even do it ourselves each year. It's that centuries-old tradition of a deep house cleaning that ushers out the long winter months and welcomes the newness of spring. There's something so refreshing and hopeful about getting to open the windows and air things out, and it can be surprising when we discover what's been lurking in corners and on windowsills for far too long.

While we're clearly talking about a physical activity here, it can also illustrate the importance of another kind of practice—a spiritual one. It can be so helpful for us to set aside a significant time (and it doesn't have to be just once a year either) to do a little housecleaning in our hearts. Because many of us live full lives in a fast-paced culture, we can get so busy checking off our to-do lists and covering our bases that we lose touch with what's happening within us. What attitudes have we picked up? What regrets are we dragging along? What worries have been collecting in our lives for so long that we forget how it feels to live free of them? "Spiritual spring cleaning" can be a game changer, and we can do it during any season of our lives!

Pursue Peace

Jesus was a Master at revealing the hidden things—the well-disguised motives, unexpressed hurts, and self-deceit people carried, often unknowingly. He knew that the longer we go without clearing out those hidden things, the more discouragement and despair we live with—even if we aren't aware of where it's coming from. That's why one of the greatest gifts we can give ourselves is a deeper look within. We can ask our loving Father to open those doors within our hearts and help us discover what's hiding there—what needs healing and confessing. Just becoming aware of those things is a big step. So, whether you've been feeling wonderful or wary about life lately, consider taking some time in a quiet place to do these three things:

1. Ask God to reveal anything that's weighing you down.
2. Spend some time prayerfully listening and write down anything that comes to your mind and heart.
3. Commit to taking one step to address whatever comes up, however that may look for you.

Pay attention to how God works in the coming days to help you clean up that clutter and live more freely and peacefully. This can be a wonderful tradition to establish, and just like that spring cleaning practice, it'll surely bring a greater sense of hope and lightness to the home that is your heart.

PAUSE FOR PRAYER

Dear Heavenly Father,

I come to You today seeking Your guidance and strength. Life often presents me with choices that test my patience, my understanding, and my faith. In those moments, Lord, help me to choose peace.

When I am faced with conflict, remind me to seek resolution with kindness and humility. When anger or frustration rises within me, fill my heart with Your calming presence. Help me to let go of grudges and replace bitterness with forgiveness. Teach me to respond to challenges with grace and to trust You in every situation.

Lord, give me the wisdom to choose thoughts that bring peace, words that build up, and actions that promote harmony. Let Your Spirit guide me, anchoring me in Your love and truth. Help me to embrace the stillness You offer, even amid life's storms.

May Your peace flow through me, influencing my relationships, my decisions, and my outlook on life. Let me be a reflection of Your peace to others, drawing them closer to You.

In Jesus's name I pray. Amen.

Finding Freedom

All the darkness in the world cannot extinguish the light of a single candle.
ST. FRANCIS OF ASSISI

Those of us who've been on this planet for any amount of time have learned that there are many things we cannot control . . . and only a few precious things that we can. This isn't usually what we want to hear, but the sooner we learn to accept this truth, the more peaceful our lives can become. Not because our circumstances change, of course, but because we surrender to the fact that, as someone once so wisely stated, "There is a God, and He is not us." (Thank heaven!) When we find ourselves in tough situations that are out of our control, we may feel fearful, trapped, resentful, and sometimes even hopeless. It can be hard to stop our heads from spinning and our hearts from hurting as we wonder why it's happening and how we're ever going to get through it. We value our freedom as human beings, and when we feel like parts of it are taken away unfairly, we struggle mightily to accept that. As we learn to use *less* energy trying to manage what isn't in our job description as human beings, we free up *more* energy for what we are actually here to do: serve God and one another in love. This is especially important to remember during discouraging times in life. Maybe we can't do a whole lot to change our conditions at the moment, but that's okay. Because there will always be a few things we *can* do—even small things—and the sooner we focus on those, the more peace we will experience.

Pursue Peace

Whether or not you're dealing with an experience that leaves you feeling out of control, there is something you can consider doing anytime you're feeling boxed in by life: *use your imagination*. It can help you shift your focus from *What can't I do?* to *What's possible for me right now?* Perhaps you're separated from someone you love for a while. And while you miss them more than you can express, there's nothing you can do to change it at the moment. So, you decide to put your energy toward nurturing a friendship that brings joy to your heart. Of course, it doesn't make things "all better," but it *can* bring some lightness to your life. Or maybe you aren't able to use your body to dance right now due to a physical limitation. Why not focus on those things you still *can* do that make your heart happy? If you want to find other ways to enjoy music, consider learning an instrument. Focus less on what you can't do and more on what you *can*. See how it feels to live more and more from that perspective. We don't often understand why God allows us to experience these tough times, but we never have to question whether He's there in the midst of them, offering us new ways to find joy in Him, regardless of our circumstances.

Meeting Your Fears

Courage doesn't always roar. Sometimes courage is the little voice at the end of the day that says I'll try again tomorrow.

MARY ANNE RADMACHER

When you think back on your childhood, you probably remember at least a few significant times when you felt very afraid. And from your adult perspective, some of those times may now seem a little "silly." Monsters under the bed, sharks in the swimming pool, something lurking in the attic . . . you get the idea. Fear is fear, after all—at any age, from any perspective. We may experience it for different reasons, but we all know how it feels. And no matter what stage of life we're in or what we're feeling afraid of, it's so helpful to meet ourselves with the kind of compassion Jesus has for us. Think about what happens when a child cries out in the night. A loving parent often responds by offering their presence. Instead of shaming that little one or dismissing their fear and telling them to "just get over it," the parent tries to understand where it's coming from. They may ask, "What happened to make you feel afraid?" And once their child has shared what's on their mind, he or she may be offered a few minutes in the rocking chair or something else to help them feel a sense of safety and reassurance.

Now, fast-forward to adulthood. We still have a loving Father who assures us wholeheartedly: "I am the Lord your God who takes hold of your right hand and says to you, 'Do not fear; I will help you'" (Isaiah 41:13 NIV). How well do we sense His presence when we need it most?

Pursue Peace

Unlike that loving parent described above, we're often quite hard on ourselves when it comes to dealing with difficult emotions. We may feel embarrassed or frustrated that we can't just "get over" something. Maybe the monster under our bed has to do with feeling inadequate in our work, expecting the worst with a health diagnosis, being worried about finances . . . the list goes on. Just because we deal with "grown-up" issues these days doesn't mean we feel any more confident than we did as children. We still need to be met with tenderness and understanding. We still need reassurance and reminders that everything will be okay. And the good news is, the Source of all those wonderful things lives within us. God's Spirit offers us all we need to feel safe and secure in His love. So, the next time you discover those uninvited worries or fears knocking on your door, instead of stuffing those feelings down or scurrying to manage them, take a moment to sit with them. Close your eyes, take a deep breath, and acknowledge God's presence calming you like the most patient, understanding, compassionate Father in the universe (because He is, you know). The more you do this, the more naturally you will be able to walk in peace, no matter what life brings.

The Art of Waiting

Patience is the calm acceptance that things can happen in a different order than the one you have in mind.

DAVID G. ALLEN

What does your patience meter look like these days? Are you one of those people who keeps opening the oven to check the cookies when you know full well they're not done? Maybe you scoot them around a bit and stare real hard, hoping that somehow, they'll turn that perfect golden-brown color right before your eyes. Sure, the timer says ten more minutes, but your sweet tooth says . . . *now*! Or maybe you're the kind of person who can just let it go and walk away. Those cookies will be done when they're done, and no amount of peeking in will change that. When it comes to having patience, most of us are somewhere in the middle, depending on the situation or season we're in. Sometimes we're able to take that age-old "let go and let God" advice and let it be. Other times, we're white-knuckling everything, determined to make it all work our way and in our time. And while checking on cookies doesn't have a significant effect on us, trusting God's timing in the bigger things does.

It can be hard to admit that we don't have much control over our circumstances. That doesn't mean we're helpless, of course; it just means we're not running the universe, and we do much better in the back seat than at the helm. When we learn to strive less and surrender more, we can find true peace in being along for the ride.

Pursue Peace

When it comes to sustaining a sense of peace on our journey, patience plays a big role. Every time we start grasping for control of those things that only God can work out in our lives, we feed our doubt that He is able and willing to take care of us. One of the most helpful things we can do for ourselves is to intentionally practice patience in the little things, so that when we're facing the not-so-little things, we've developed spiritual strength to handle them. This begins by simply noticing when we feel anxious or frustrated by something we can't control—long lines at the store, stubborn stoplights, maybe a person who's talking our ear off when we *really just want to get home*! Practice taking a deep breath, come back to the moment, and shift your thoughts toward gratitude. *Thank You, Lord, for Your perfect timing.* As that simple shift becomes a habit, you'll notice yourself relaxing and breathing more easily in everyday situations that used to stress you out. And, most importantly, when you face those more significant situations that could cause doubt and discouragement to take over, you may surprise yourself with the patience muscles you've developed. God's timing is God's timing, in the big and little things, and the more we lean in to that, the greater our peace and contentment will be.

Growing Brighter

Hope is being able to see that there is light despite all the darkness.

DESMOND TUTU

One thing we all share as God's creatures is the need for light—both the sunshiny kind and the spiritual kind! We're just drawn to it, whether it be the morning sun beaming through the kitchen window or the warm love of Jesus shining through the heart of a friend. If we find ourselves spending too much time in the dark—of any kind—we can really start to feel it. Our hearts weren't created to live in the shadows; they were made to thrive in the radiance of God's goodness and truth.

There's a popular science fair project that illustrates that wonderfully, and it's something we can remember during the ups and downs of our spiritual journeys. Here's how it goes: A seed is planted in a small container, which is set in the bottom of a big box. The box has been turned into a maze, filled with obstacles, with the seed at the very bottom and a hole cut all the way up at the top, where light is coming through. Over time, as the plant grows, it naturally finds its way around the barriers of the maze and up toward the hole. Why? Because it was created to reach toward the light, and no matter what gets in its way in the darkness, that plant will not be deterred. It's not about how big those barriers are or how many twists and turns that vine has to take; it's simply about being irresistibly drawn toward the brightness above. And isn't that how our journey happens too?

Pursue Peace

We each grow through the maze of this life differently, but the most important thing for all of us is not the challenges we have to overcome but the fact that we have a very present, loving Creator who's always there, willing to illuminate our path if we are paying attention.

Consider the verses below—just a few of the many messages about light in God's Word. Does any message in particular speak to your heart today about your own journey?

- *You are all children of the light and children of the day. We do not belong to the night or to the darkness* (I Thessalonians 5:5 NIV).
- *The Lord is my light and my salvation—whom shall I fear? The Lord is the stronghold of my life—of whom shall I be afraid?* (Psalm 27:1 NIV).
- *The city does not need the sun or the moon to shine on it, for the glory of God gives it light, and the Lamb is its lamp* (Revelation 21:23 NIV).

Consider writing a note for your future self to read when things feel discouraging. How would you remind yourself to look for the light in tough times? We all need that nudge once in a while, and who better to give your heart a pep talk than the person who knows you best? You!

Finding Balance

Almost everything will work again if you unplug it for a few minutes, including you.

ANNE LAMOTT

Most of us have experienced the feeling of bone-deep exhaustion at some point. We may each arrive at the end of our ropes in different ways, but when we get there, we may wonder how we'll ever pull ourselves back up again, and how the world is possibly going to go on without us in the meantime. We have people to show up for, after all! And stuff to make, and things to attend! But just the thought of putting more effort toward anything feels quite overwhelming at the moment. The longer we live in that tension between "*I can't do this anymore*" and "*I gotta keep going somehow*," the more depleted we become. And, lest we forget, we can't pour from an empty cup. We cannot be any good for anyone else without taking the time to lean in to the loving arms of our Father and fill up on His rest, peace, and love. We also need to remember that we usually fall into those exhaustion traps gradually. We take baby steps toward them by shaving off some sleep time here and there, ignoring that red flag our bodies have been waving, taking on one project too many when we know full well it's not in our best interest, but . . . we think it's such a good cause, and maybe this time we'll develop some sort of superpower that pulls us through! We might imagine our Creator standing nearby in those moments, watching us make those unhealthy choices, shaking His head lovingly and waiting for us to utter the one word that'll surely come from our hearts soon: "*HELP!*"

Pursue Peace

Few of us want to hear this these days because it sounds so impractical and impossible, but . . . *we need to find ways to unplug regularly.* For example, setting aside time for quiet walks, designating one evening a week sans devices, or allowing for naps or peaceful times of prayer or quiet activities can fill our hearts and bring us back to ourselves. *We must be intentional about taking care of us* because no one else knows what we need like we do. In fact, we don't even know what we need like God does! That's why asking Him for little ways to find greater peace and balance in our lives is a great place to start. If you are experiencing one of those "end of your rope" times right now, be tender with yourself. Try to care for yourself like you would someone in your life whom you dearly love. Become okay with saying "no" to others for a while so you can say "yes" to you. Every time you make a healthy choice in your life, you recognize your God-given worth. When you're tempted to push yourself too far or deny yourself the rest you need, remember that the world will keep turning and you'll be better equipped to handle whatever life throws at you when you prioritize caring for yourself.

PAUSE FOR PRAYER

Heavenly Father,

I come to You with a heart that longs for Your peace to guide my life. In this busy and uncertain world, I often feel overwhelmed by the choices before me. Lord, I ask for Your calming presence to fill my mind and heart, quieting the anxieties that cloud my judgment.

Help me to choose peace in every situation. Teach me to pause, to listen to Your voice, and to follow the path You have laid before me. When decisions arise, grant me wisdom and discernment to make choices that honor You and bring harmony to my life and to those around me.

Lord, replace my doubts and fears with the confidence of knowing You are in control. Give me the courage to walk away from conflict and the strength to seek reconciliation when needed. Help me to trust in Your timing and to rest in the assurance that Your plans are for my good.

Let Your peace rule in my heart and guide my decisions so I may live a life pleasing to You.

In Jesus's name I pray. Amen.

Change Your Mind

There's only one corner of the universe you can be certain of improving, and that's your own self.
ALDOUS HUXLEY

How do you feel when you hear the words: *That's just the way I am*, or *That's just the way it is*? It may be in the middle of an argument when one person is asking for the other to do something differently. Or during a discussion about the challenging circumstances someone is facing. There's a sense of defeat in those statements—an assumption that nothing's going to change, so why bother trying? Yes, acknowledging the reality of things is important. But God would surely remind us, when we are facing those seemingly impossible situations, to keep our hearts open to possibility—trusting that He is working in the midst of it all in His way and in His time. Meanwhile, we can remember this: *Even if nothing appears to be changing in that difficult relationship or situation, we always have the freedom to choose how we will experience it.* We can be inspired by Paul's invitation in Romans 12:2 (TLB): "Don't copy the behavior and customs of this world, but be a new and different person with a fresh newness in all you do and think. Then you will learn from your own experience how His ways will really satisfy you." It's true: we can always choose hope over despair, peace over worry, grace over grumbling, gratitude over complaint. Sure, it takes some practice, but as it becomes more natural for us, we will have the capacity for greater joy and satisfaction within us, regardless of what we are facing in our lives.

Pursue Peace

Try this exercise to help illustrate the power of your thoughts in determining how you experience your life. Find a familiar place—maybe a room in your home, your backyard, your office—anywhere you spend a good amount of time. Now look around that place and find every negative thing about it that you possibly can. Maybe it's dusty, there's a stain on the rug, the grass needs mowed, that computer is outdated . . . you get the idea. Then, close your eyes for a moment, take a deep breath, clear your mind, open your eyes, and look around again. This time, look for all the good. The sun is shining. You're blessed to have a safe, comfortable home. There is no end to the blessings you can count. In fact, you may notice that you can list more good things than bad. God's gifts are infinite; we simply fail to recognize them sometimes in our day-to-day lives. So, back to those tough relationships and situations. How have you been thinking about them? How would you *like* to think about them? Remember, you *always* have the freedom to choose your experience. And you can trust that God is always working in your circumstances, and even before you witness the fruit of that, you can choose to enjoy the journey.

Your Biggest Moments

There's never been a single moment when God was not with you.

ANONYMOUS

At times in history, much of the world seemed to pause, hold their collective breath, and acknowledge the immensity of a moment. If you lived through the 1980s, for instance, you probably remember where you were on that fateful day when the space shuttle *Challenger* was launched—a mission that never reached its destination. Or maybe you, or someone you know, was blessed to witness a more joyous occasion in space: those first triumphant steps of Neil Armstrong on the moon. Something about the communal response of hundreds, thousands, or even millions of people makes an event feel very significant—and for good reason!

Some defining moments and turning points in history can affect all of us for generations to come. But those more private, monumental moments that we experience as individuals are just as earth-shattering for us, personally, even if they don't happen for all the world to see. And while our loved ones may have witnessed and shared in some of them, realize that, try as they might, no one else on the planet can understand exactly how it feels to be in our shoes because, well . . . they're *our* shoes! It's tough when big things are happening for us (both the wonderful and not-so-wonderful) and nobody seems to comprehend the immensity of it all like we do. Guess who *does* understand it though . . . every detail? Our audience of One. The One who made us and knows us, inside and out.

Pursue Peace

Here's a simple, healing thing you can do to remind yourself of God's presence throughout your life, especially in those times when you may have felt unnoticed, unappreciated, or just plain alone. First, take out your journal or a sketch pad—this is something you can write about or draw if you want to get creative! Make a list of (or sketch out) a few of the most monumental moments in your life that you can remember—both happy and difficult times—whether they were obvious to others or known only to you. Recall as many details as you can . . . how it happened, who was there, what you felt, how it affected your life moving forward, maybe in ways you didn't even realize at the time. Acknowledging the significance of what we've been through can be a helpful, healing thing, and sometimes it gives us some closure we didn't even realize we needed. When you are finished sharing, remind yourself once again of God's nearness, of His deep and complete understanding of your heart, and of His commitment to be there for all your moments, great and small, for all eternity.

The Light of Hope

Hope is a passion for the possible.
SØREN KIERKEGAARD

When we look back on our collective history—the history of humankind—we can surely see those times when darkness seemed to dominate. But if we could somehow zoom in very closely, we would also be able to see, against the backdrop of that darkness, points of light that shine like stars in the night sky. And those points of light would be the people who never gave up hope in the midst of our world's most difficult times. They're the ones who dared to dream of brighter days when others had decided that things would never get better—the ones who kept trying, kept taking small steps toward positive change, even if no one believed it made any difference . . . even if their efforts went unnoticed and unappreciated. Who knows what kind of world we'd live in today if they had not each done their small but mighty part?

It seems that our beautiful Creator placed a treasure within each of us when He made us, and that was the capacity for hope. To hope is to believe in what we can't yet see, and to trust that, as Jesus reminds us in Matthew 19:26 (NLT), "Humanly speaking, it is impossible. But with God everything is possible."

Pursue Peace

God is calling people everywhere, every day to shine His light of hope for the world. Here are two things we can do when we find ourselves feeling discouraged about the state of our community or our world.

We can become more intentionally aware of the people who are doing all they can to share the hope of Christ around us. We can be inspired by their courage and compassion as we witness the ways they follow God's leading to serve those He brings into their lives.

We can ask in prayer how we, too, might be a light for others. Even if we don't sense a specific response right away, we can trust that in His time, God will reveal those answers to us. He may nudge us toward some very down-to-earth actions we can take. He might simply whisper to our hearts in the moment: "*That waitress could really use a word of encouragement today*" or "*See that teacher? He's overwhelmed, and he needs to know he's making a difference.*" Regardless of when or how He calls us, we always have the choice whether to answer that call. He loves us no matter what we choose, but He knows the joy it can bring to our hearts when we step into those opportunities to light the world with His love.

Your Quiet Place

Deep within us all there is an amazing inner sanctuary . . . a holy place.

THOMAS RAYMOND KELLY

Here's a wonderful thing about you that you may need reminding of from time to time: there is a part of you, deep within, that is absolutely *untouchable*. No one in all creation gets access to that part of you . . . no one except your Maker. We're talking about the "you" behind your thoughts; beyond your beliefs and your expectations are your actions. We're talking about the unique and beautiful soul you are that God breathed into existence and called "good." The one looking out through your eyes, laughing your laugh, and learning to live as a spiritual being in a physical world. Yes, God gave you a body that allows you to experience His creation in countless ways. He gave you a mind to make sense of things, to create and imagine and believe. But beneath all of that is the heart of you, made in His image, enlivened by His Spirit, loved and protected from every force that would seek to dim your light.

Does this mean you feel the truth of that all the time? No, of course not. Does it destroy every doubt and fear you face as you navigate your everyday life? Nope. But the more often you pause to remember who (and Whose) you are, the more courage, hope, and untouchable joy you can experience in life. Because we know those things don't come from the outside, as much as the world would try to convince us otherwise. They come from deep within.

Pursue Peace

Here's an exercise that can help remind you of that peaceful place at your center, where you can experience God's presence deeply, beyond all the noise. Find a quiet spot and a comfortable position, then set a timer for ten minutes with the sole intention to just *be*. That may seem like a short amount of time, but when your goal is to do absolutely nothing but show up and breathe, it can feel like an eternity! Sitting quietly makes us very aware of how noisy our minds can be. But it also reminds us of this powerful truth: *We are much more than our thoughts.* The more we learn to simply observe our train of thought in those times of quiet, the more naturally it will come and go. Then, when we find ourselves out in the world, encountering the circumstances and relationships that usually hijack our minds and cause us to feel upset or discouraged, we can experience them with more peace and acceptance. We can take a deep breath, let those thoughts go, and return to that awareness of God's Spirit within us as we receive the promise found in Isaiah: "You will keep in perfect peace all who trust in You, all whose thoughts are fixed on You!" (Isaiah 26:3 NLT).

The Gift of Discomfort

Outside our comfort zone . . .
is where we experience the true awesomeness of God.
LYSA TERKEURST

Okay, take a deep breath before reading this because it's a tough pill to swallow: *Discomfort is a very important experience in our lives.* "What?!?" we might exclaim, recalling that awful rainy campout that ended our outdoorsy career, those too-tight pants we can't seem to let go of, or even the awkwardness of running into someone at the grocery store who makes us feel, well . . . *uncomfortable.*

There's something about discomfort that wakes us up, forces us to shift out of autopilot and into our bodies, and frankly, just reminds us how very human we are. Wouldn't you know that God, in His infinite wisdom, happens to have the perfect recipe for using discomfort for our growth. Whether it be facing an illness, the intimidating learning curve of a new job, lack of sleep due to that infant who's suddenly taken over our house—most of us are facing at least something in our lives that we wish was easier. And while our Creator doesn't "send" things to hurt us, He absolutely uses *everything* to help us.

Whatever discomfort you are experiencing in your life today—whether it feels heavily burdensome or just mildly annoying—He is always inviting you to "grow through what you go through." Whether or not you decide to accept that invitation is, of course, up to you.

Pursue Peace

Here's a challenge that can help increase your self-awareness about your own "comfort zones" and inspire you to expand your life experience. Find one thing to do that makes you more than a little uncomfortable this week—something that will require some courage and determination. It could be making a phone call to someone you've felt distant from lately, choosing to fast for part of a day, or trying a new activity you've felt very intimidated by. The important thing is that your experience causes you to become more aware of your thoughts and feelings in those moments. Ask yourself things like: *Why have I avoided this? What am I resisting, and can I allow myself to stay present long enough to feel it?* And most importantly, *How might God use this discomfort to help me grow?* You may gain a deeper sense of courage within yourself or greater compassion for what others go through in life. You might become more aware of feelings you try to avoid. *Discomfort is only a bad thing if we choose to experience it that way.* Allow God to work in it, and you may be pleasantly surprised at what He shows you in the process.

PAUSE FOR PRAYER

Dear Lord Jesus,

I come to You with a humble heart, seeking Your guidance and strength to pursue peace in my life. You are the God of peace, the One who calms storms and restores order. Lord, I ask that You fill my heart with Your presence, helping me to choose peace in every moment.

When I am tempted to respond with anger or frustration, remind me of Your patience and love. Teach me to let go of pride, resentment, and fear, and instead embrace humility, forgiveness, and trust in You. Show me how to be a peacemaker in my relationships, to speak words that build up rather than tear down, and to act with kindness even when it's difficult.

Guide my thoughts and actions, Lord, so they reflect Your peace. Help me to seek You first in all things, trusting that Your wisdom will lead me in the right direction. Strengthen my faith to rely on Your promises and to rest in the assurance that You are always with me.

May my pursuit of peace bring glory to Your name, drawing others closer to You. Thank You for being my source of true peace.

In Jesus's name I pray. Amen.

Sacred Seeing

God's purpose shines through everything; it's up to us to discover it.

ANONYMOUS

When you go outside and look up on a clear night, do you see pictures and patterns among the stars, or do you see random, brilliant points of light scattered across the dark sky? The answer to that question likely depends on what you've learned throughout your life. At some point, you may have been taught about constellations. Many of us grew up hearing stories that have been passed down for generations, inviting us to connect the dots and imagine things like those five stars there on the horizon forming an animal or a cross or a bow and arrow. Once someone points out a pattern or connection that we're able to see clearly, it's often hard to unsee. We can walk outside and tell ourselves we're just looking at a bunch of unrelated dots, but those stories created pictures in our minds, and these minds of ours are quite impressionable! This is a wonderful thing to remember when we're struggling with a sense of purpose or meaning in our lives. God's Word is like our constellation map: it's our forever reminder that we live in a much larger story, that nothing is random, that every little thing matters—and not only that, but it's all part of a beautiful picture that's slowly coming into view over time. When we find ourselves doubting that truth, we can often trace it back to our connection with Him. We need to draw close and be reminded, once again, that the dots in our lives are connected by His design, even when we don't always understand how.

Pursue Peace

How can we remind ourselves that every detail matters in God's design? Proverbs 3:5–6 describes three things we can do regularly in our lives:

1. *Trust in the Lord with all your heart.*

That's a lot of trust He's asking for! But we know He is more than worthy of it. And it doesn't happen for us all at once, of course. Trust grows moment by moment, both through our everyday experiences and in the middle of those more epic events we encounter.

2. *Do not lean on your own understanding.*

It isn't easy to give our own understanding a back seat, but there's a deeper sense of knowing that comes only from our Maker.

3. *In all your ways acknowledge Him.*

To "acknowledge" means "to admit the existence or truth of." Our life experiences can be so much more meaningful and satisfying when we acknowledge God's presence in the midst of them. This can be as quiet as a prayer whispered in our hearts or as exuberant as the praise we shout from the rooftops.

This passage ends with the promise that "He will make your paths straight" (NIV). We can trust that every step we take has purpose, and He knows exactly where He's leading us. There's a lot of peace to be found in that truth.

Just Be You

Live your life for an audience of One.

ANONYMOUS

Reputation can be a tricky thing. If you've ever been the subject of hurtful gossip or someone has intentionally tried to convince others of something negative about you, then you know exactly what that means. Many of us were raised in families who valued having a "good name," and for good reason! Whether it be in friendships, jobs, ministry positions, or other relationships, people can be reluctant to build connections with someone who is generally considered untrustworthy or unreliable. And we, as followers of Jesus, called to speak truth, model integrity, and love well—we do what we can to live with good character. *But* . . . that doesn't always guarantee that we can keep ourselves out of the rumor mill. Sometimes it's just out of our hands. And as hard as it is to admit, there are people in the world—and sometimes in our own lives—who are determined, for whatever reason, to drag us down. It may be their own insecurities, envy, misdirected anger—only God knows, and it's really not our job to figure it out. But what we *can* control is our own thoughts, our intentions, and our actions. The more we keep our focus on those things and off other people's interpretations and opinions about our lives . . . the better off we will be.

Pursue Peace

Even if you aren't dealing right now with someone else's judgment or misunderstanding, people everywhere are hurt by others' negative opinions and accusations. One way we can be a light in this area is to model integrity. Our integrity doesn't hinge on anyone else's ideas about us; it is our desire to live right from the inside out because that's what God calls us to do. Not only does integrity help protect us from the sting of others' criticism by giving us a more solid sense of ourselves, but it also keeps us from trying to put up a false front to impress them. There's no need for a façade when we have nothing to hide. Pay attention in the coming days to how you feel from the inside out. Are your decisions and actions coming from your heart, or are they heavily influenced by the way others might perceive you? And what happens when you hear someone speaking negatively about another person? Let's be the light for others to live kindly and authentically. And be encouraged if you're the one feeling mistreated or misunderstood. Your loving Father knows the whole truth of you, and He gently reminds you that your heart will always be what matters most to Him.

Expect the Unexpected

Every happening, great and small, is a parable whereby God speaks to us, and the art of life is to get the message.

MALCOLM MUGGERIDGE

We don't have to spend much time in the New Testament to notice that Jesus often spoke in parables. They're stories anyone can relate to, regardless of status or human intelligence; they challenge people to think in new ways about timeless truths; and, perhaps most importantly, parables just have a way of entering our hearts first . . . before our brains have time to fit them into a structure or system that we're already comfortable with. In short: *Jesus had a backdoor way of reaching people.* That's how He was able to enter a culture where many folks had become bound by religious rules and blinded by self-righteousness, and He blew it up lovingly from the inside out. And like those people He lived among, we sometimes find ourselves spending more time in our heads than our hearts too. We can tell when that starts to happen, in fact, because we start looking around for it—usually through the "front door" of our lives, in all those expected ways we've come to know Him. But we may soon discover that He's been knocking on the *back doors* of our hearts all along. Just like Jesus did through the telling of those parables, God is always inviting us into new ways of experiencing Him, and often He will use those times when we've felt spiritually "meh" to be catalysts for our growth.

Pursue Peace

Because we are all created uniquely, our Maker knows we each have different ways of experiencing His presence. He also knows that to grow in our understanding and awareness of Him in our daily lives, we must be nudged out of our comfort zones. Sometimes that means letting one well run dry so we'll seek out another. We're constantly being invited to grow in Him and become aware of Him in new ways. Sometimes that feels quite uncomfortable. If you're facing a time of not feeling God's nearness, here are a few simple steps you can take.

1. *Remember the truth.* No matter what your experience is at the moment, He is as near to you as He has ever been, and He will never, ever leave you.
2. *Ask for help.* Ask Him to help you understand what's making you feel distant or "meh" about your connection. Is there something you need to look at? Are you paying attention?
3. *Open your heart.* Be intentional about looking for Him in your daily life and know that He surely delights in that. Your heart was designed to seek Him, and if you are open to it, He will show up in ways you never imagined.

Living Well

One day you will look back and see that all along you were blooming.

MORGAN HARPER NICHOLS

It's not surprising to learn that people who live the longest tend to share a list of common traits. And while some of those traits can vary, most can be traced right back to biblical truth. We're talking about more than just clean livin', although that's certainly a factor when it comes to helping our bodies thrive into our later years. But studies also reveal that a positive, hopeful outlook on life is one of the main determiners of longevity. Nearly three thousand years ago, King Solomon declared: "A cheerful heart is good medicine, but a crushed spirit dries up the bones" (Proverbs 17:22 NIV). He was definitely onto something! But what we can sometimes forget is that a cheerful heart takes intention. Most people who are known as "glass-half-full" folks didn't get there by accident. They chose it, and they keep choosing it every day. Sure, genetics may affect our disposition to some degree, but there's something even more powerful determining how we see the world: *the power of our own free will.* We always have the freedom to choose what we'll focus on in our lives. And it's not a one-and-done decision. It's a daily turning of our hearts toward all that's good and true, no matter what the day brings. It's easy to be cheerful when the sun is out, but when the storms come? That's when we find out what we're really made of. Those positive people we admire, who have learned to look for silver linings—it's quite likely they've had to experience some pretty tough times in order to find out what it takes to rise above it all.

Pursue Peace

A beautiful life doesn't happen by accident; we choose it one thought at a time, one action at a time, one day at a time. And that takes some real intention, especially in the more difficult seasons we go through. We must remember that no matter what we're facing, we are always free to shift our focus toward "what is true, and honorable, and right, and pure, and lovely, and admirable" (Philippians 4:8 NLT). And in doing so, we allow our most difficult times to bring forth unexpected goodness. That sounds lovely in theory, but how do we walk that out in real life? Well, first of all, we start today. Even if it means starting small . . . even if there's nothing big and ugly staring us in the face at the moment. Each time we redirect a thought from fear to faith, each time we choose a word of affirmation over a complaint, each time we lift someone up instead of discouraging them—we're adding a brick to that beautiful life we're building. As we heed the wisdom of Ephesians 4:23 (CEV)—"Let the Spirit change your way of thinking"—those good thoughts will grow into actions . . . that's just how it works! And so one day, we will be able to look back and see a life well-lived.

Behind the Scenes

Never be afraid to trust an unknown future to a known God.
CORRIE TEN BOOM

Have you ever been sitting near a window with sunlight streaming through, and you suddenly notice tiny flecks floating in the air? It may look like dust or bits of fuzz, but whatever it is, you didn't notice it until the sun's angle was just right and revealed the presence of something you had no idea was drifting about. Then, you start to realize that those itty-bitty particles are floating around everywhere in your house; you just don't usually see them. Similarly, just because we can't see something all the time doesn't mean it's not there affecting us somehow.

Our spiritual lives are no different . . . and that is a helpful, hopeful thing to remember. We might be seeking God's guidance in a particular situation and wondering if we'll ever find our way. We could be praying for relief from an ongoing struggle. And if we're honest, many of us have thrown up our hands and wondered, *Is anyone really listening at all?* Of course, we know the answer to that; we know that God is good, and real, and so very present—even on days when we just can't feel it. But sometimes we do need a reminder that it's all going to be okay in the end, even if we don't quite understand how.

It can be tough to understand why God keeps some things hidden from our view as long as He does. Our human perspective is so limited, and that's why He asks us to trust His heart and His timing. As Romans 8:28 reminds us, He's always working for the highest good of those who love Him. And that includes *you*.

Pursue Peace

So, what can you do during those times of waiting and wondering how things are going to work out? Let's return for a moment to those dust particles floating around. Remember: They're always there, but we only glimpse them when they're revealed by the sunlight. We will never see *all* of them at the same time, but we can see a *few* of them when conditions are right. The same is true for us spiritually. When you're feeling discouraged about a situation or season in your life, take a moment to ask your heavenly Father for some glimmers of hope. Ask Him to help you believe in what you can't see right now. Remember: Just because you're dealing with doubt doesn't mean you don't trust Him. It just means you need to feel His nearness most in times of uncertainty, like a child who reaches for her father's hand. Ask Him for that reassurance and be open to all the ways He might provide it. Even if the bigger things are still being worked out behind the scenes, the silver linings He offers are always available to those of us with eyes to see.

PAUSE FOR PRAYER

Heavenly Father,

I come before You today feeling the weight of stress and uncertainty in my life. Lord, You are my refuge and strength, a constant help in times of trouble. I ask for Your peace to wash over me, calming my heart and quieting my mind. Remind me, Lord, that You are in control, even when life feels overwhelming.

Father, fill me with hope during this season of struggle. Help me to fix my eyes on You and to trust in Your promises. Remind me that Your plans for me are good, plans to give me a future filled with hope. When I feel discouraged, lift my spirit and help me see Your light shining through the darkness.

Lord, I also ask for Your comfort. Wrap me in Your loving embrace and remind me that I am never alone. Strengthen me with Your presence and provide the reassurance I need to face each day. Guide my steps, give me clarity in my decisions, and grant me rest in Your arms.

Thank You, Lord, for being my source of peace, hope, and comfort. I trust in You and Your unfailing love.

In Jesus's name I pray. Amen.

From Head to Heart

Art is a reflection of God's creativity, an evidence that we are made in the image of God.
FRANCIS SCHAEFFER

Whether or not you would describe yourself as a "creative" person, it's likely that some form of art has inspired you at some point in your life. It could be anything from live theater to paintings to gardening to exquisite culinary presentations. Creativity is everywhere, and unless we are determined to resist it, something will usually find its way in to touch us somehow. Why might this be important in the big picture of our lives? Because it helps to give us greater balance between our heads and our hearts—especially those among us who tend to overthink or often feel a bit "trapped" in our minds. We get a kind of tunnel vision, and things start to look very dark and serious. We see less beauty and possibility, and we experience more worry and fear, and it can be tough to free ourselves from that cycle once it begins. Those are the moments when we most need to take that eighteen-inch (or so) journey from our heads to our hearts. We need a greater sense of hope and lightness and freedom. And a wonderful way to get us there is creativity. This could be as simple as listening to an uplifting song, making something with our hands, or looking at a book of beautiful photography. God seems to have designed us in such a way that art—in whatever form we're drawn to—is able to bring us back to the moment, refresh us, and offer us a respite from whatever is weighing us down.

Pursue Peace

Most of us have heard of or read Jesus's well-known invitation for His followers to "become like little children" (see Matthew 18:3 NIV). Children are generally more open-minded, less self-conscious, and able to be present in the moment, unlike many adults who are constantly evaluating, planning, dreading . . . you get the picture. This is why the youngest (and most young-hearted) among us are so much freer to create. It's also why those of us who struggle most with worry and overthinking can benefit greatly from allowing art—in whatever form uniquely speaks to us—to offer us a recess from our "big, important" thoughts. So here's your challenge, should you choose to accept it: Find one form of art to enjoy in the week ahead. Set aside even a half hour (set a timer if it helps you to let go a little easier), and let it be a time of pure enjoyment. Whether you're observing someone else's creations or experiencing your own, just be aware of God's presence with you in the moment and know that He delights in your childlike spirit. Art can help to heal and bring hope to our hearts in tough times. After all, we're made in the image of the ultimate Creator. Surely His plans for us include some unique and beautiful creations of our own.

Spinning Our Wheels

If you change nothing, nothing changes.
JOYCE BROTHERS

Have you ever heard yourself say something like, "*I just feel so stuck right now*"? That feeling visits all of us, in one way or another, at different times in our lives. Whether it's a goal we're aiming for, a relationship we're working on, or just life in general, we sometimes reach a point when we just don't sense any forward movement or positive change; we can't see the path ahead clearly, and we're simply tired of standing still. At those times, we ask ourselves: Whom do we trust? Where do we start? Which step do we take first?

Thankfully, as the psalmist reminds us in Psalm 121, we don't have to scramble for solutions. Our help comes from an infinite, loving Creator who has all we need to thrive: "I lift up my eyes to the mountains—where does my help come from? My help comes from the Lord, the Maker of heaven and earth" (Psalm 121:1–2 NIV). When our frustrated hearts are calling for our attention, we don't have to head down that rabbit hole of worry, wondering how we'll ever get things moving in a hopeful direction again. We simply need to stop and ask for help.

Pursue Peace

If you've ever driven a car into deep snow, mud, or sand and found yourself spinning your wheels, you eventually realize that it's pointless to do the same thing over and over again and expect different results. The same goes with those frustrating situations in our lives. The greatest gift we can give ourselves in those times is to stop and say a simple prayer for help. The moment we invite God to meet us in that rut is the first step toward our freedom from it. So how about your life right now? Do you feel like you're spinning your wheels somehow? Any situations or relationships that just feel stuck? If so, take a few moments to write those things down and ask God for one small step you could take toward change. It may be a nudge to switch up your daily routine in some way, inspiration to pick up the phone and make a call, or maybe even to seek out the wisdom of someone who's been there. Your job is simply to listen with your heart and trust His guidance. Even if nothing changes today, you can live with that wonderful sense of hope that He's always working. And one day you will look back and see how He brought you out of that place one prayer and one step at a time.

Helping Hearts

Positive thinking must be followed by positive doing.

JOHN MAXWELL

There's a lot going on in this world of ours. Of course, we know that has always been true—we just haven't always had twenty-four-hour news cycles reminding us of this fact. A few hundred years ago, people couldn't see what was happening on the other side of the globe; they were more concerned with what was going on right in front of them. And while we have the gift of being more broadly connected today, unfortunately we also have the burden of information overload, and that can include a lot of negativity. We may find ourselves weeding through discouraging headlines, observing hurtful online exchanges between those with different convictions, and maybe even just wishing things didn't feel so heavy. It can be a tough environment in which to stay positive, but God always makes a way, if we're paying attention. He gives us each unique opportunities to find glimmers of hope and share them with others, right where we are. In fact, whenever we pray for the "world" we can remember that we're part of it—and we're part of the answer to that prayer too. Every little step we take to bring hope makes a difference. Every time we choose gratitude over complaint, joy over discouragement, belief over despair—it matters, infinitely. Not because the whole world is suddenly changed by our small daily actions, but because God is able to take those mustard seeds of effort and grow them into beautiful things, as only He can do.

Pursue Peace

When Fred Rogers (the man known for creating the heartwarming children's television show *Mister Rogers' Neighborhood*) was a boy, and he would see scary things in the news, his mother would tell him, "Look for the helpers. You will always find people who are helping." She was teaching him how to shift his focus away from fear and toward peace and hope . . . and it's a lesson we all can surely benefit from. Give it a try in the next few days. When headlines loom or negative chatter persists, challenge yourself to rise above it and look for the hopeful things that are happening around you. They can be very simple: a barista brightening days with a warm smile, a story about a compassionate pet rescue, a neighbor giving a hand to change a tire. As you observe those day brighteners, ask God to help you be one of them. The more often you take those opportunities to lift up your fellow humans, the more you'll be reminded that you aren't alone in doing so. There are others being called to shine His light alongside you. No matter what the news says or what the day brings, the helpers will always be there, and you can be one of them.

Stop, Surrender, Be Still

God is always making a way, even when you don't see one.

ANONYMOUS

Have you ever heard these words, often shared to encourage those who are facing battles in their lives: "The Lord will fight for you; you need only to be still" (Exodus 14:14 NIV)? We can all be encouraged to trust that God is absolutely able and willing to handle anything. Especially those things that feel impossible or overwhelming to us. Of course, God's *not* saying, "Hey, start a fight, and I'll finish it for you." But He *is* saying, in essence: "That hard thing you're facing? I'm in it with you, all the way. Just let me take the lead." That message was given as He led the Israelites through a life of slavery and into freedom. And in the same way, He speaks to people throughout history (and that includes us) who are walking through the most discouraging, disappointing, or even downright fearful times of our lives.

Our battles happen for many reasons; we may have even had a hand in starting them, or we may have been blindsided by circumstances beyond our control. Regardless, the thing that matters most is that we recognize our need to surrender it all to our Maker. And as we do, we must remember that when He fights for us, the victory may happen very differently than we envision, but it will always happen for the highest good of all who trust in Him.

Pursue Peace

Whether or not you're going through something big right now, there's a simple thing you can do to remind yourself of God's presence and guidance in any battles you'll face in life. Find a place to display these three instructions where you can see them often: *Stop. Surrender. Be still.*

1. *Stop.* When you realize you're facing something that's bigger than you, out of your hands, or seemingly impossible to make it through, stop and remember you're not meant to face it alone.
2. *Surrender.* Here is where we acknowledge that there's only One who truly understands this battle of ours, and He will provide all we need to get through it.
3. *Be still.* Being still doesn't mean we stop trying or pretend it's all good. It *does* mean that we turn our hearts toward God again and again in the middle of our struggles and soak in His presence. And when our minds kick into high gear wondering how in the world it's all going to work out . . . we breathe deeply and say, "God's got this," and we mean it. The more we surrender, the more we make room for peace.

Our God still shows up in unimaginable ways to bring us victory over all we face!

All We'll Ever Need

May the God of hope fill you with all joy and peace as you trust in Him.
ROMANS 15:13 NIV

The Bible calls Jesus Christ our hope in many ways. However, He is not only the hope of the Bible; Jesus is the hope of our *now*, of our every day—He's our very real and present hope. He's the One whose Spirit lives within us in this moment, tenderly loving, graciously guiding, and holding us reassuringly. The hope we have in Christ is unlike any other because it never runs out. He is eternal, and once we have given our hearts to Him, we are inseparable. That means no circumstance can be challenging enough, no mistake can be grave enough, no despair can be deep enough to take His love from us. This is vital to remember in our darkest hours, which we all face in our own ways. Even when we can't sense it; even when we feel particularly doubtful, angry, frustrated, or exasperated; even those times when we just want to cry out, *Why???* (and sometimes even *do*), He is there with a very personal and steadfast love that *does not change one bit.*

Let that truth be your anchor, no matter what you face. The hope you have in Him will outlast every other thing you experience in this life. In fact, it will outlast your life on this earth and carry you into that bright future where "what God has planned for people who love Him is more than eyes have seen or ears have heard. It has never even entered our minds!" (I Corinthians 2:9 CEV).

Pursue Peace

Here's one question to ask yourself that can be both eye-opening and inspiring: *What am I putting my hope in these days?*

To what things, experiences, or people do you look for a sense of well-being in your daily life? Of course, it's not a bad thing at all for us to own things, to enjoy experiences, and to invest in relationships—these are God's wonderful gifts to us! But it's important to stay aware of just how much we allow them to determine our happiness. We all know that nothing is guaranteed; we could wake up tomorrow without whatever it is we're depending on today. But there's not one day of your life when you will wake up without your greatest, most dependable Source of hope—God's Spirit within you. Unlike anything (or anyone) else, He is here to stay, without fail, forever. That's why cultivating your relationship with Him is the single greatest thing you can do to create a deeply joyful, peaceful, and satisfying life. So, thank God for all the good things, experiences, and people He's blessed you with in your life. Celebrate them. Keep enjoying them. Just remind yourself often that the Giver is infinitely greater than the gifts, and all you ever need will be found in Him.

PAUSE FOR PRAYER

Dear Heavenly Father,

I come to You, seeking the peace that only You can provide. My heart is heavy, and my mind is restless, filled with worries and thoughts that keep me from finding rest. Lord, You are the giver of perfect peace, the One who calms the storms within me. I ask that You quiet my heart and still my mind so that I may rest in Your presence.

Help me, Lord, to release my worries to You. Remind me that You are in control of all things and that I can trust You with every burden I carry. Teach me to let go of the things I cannot change and to surrender my fears and anxieties into Your capable hands.

Father, surround me with Your comfort in this moment. Fill my heart with the assurance of Your love, protection, and provision. Replace my restlessness with a deep sense of calm, and let Your peace guard my heart and mind as I rest. May I rise up from this time of prayer renewed and refreshed, ready to face life again with a strengthened faith and confidence in You.

Thank You, Lord, for being my refuge and strength. I rest in Your care and trust in You.

In Jesus's name I pray. Amen.

The Source of True Comfort

Snuggle in God's arms. . . . let Him cradle you, comfort you, reassure you of His all-sufficient power and love.

KAY ARTHUR

Comfort comes to us in many forms, and we all have unique ways of experiencing it. We may feel the need for it more at certain times in our lives than at other times. But one thing is certain for every person seeking solace today: it is found most deeply in the very real presence of God. There are no requirements for receiving the divine rest and reassurance He offers. No boxes to check, no favor to earn, and no need to measure up. We simply accept the daily invitation to draw close to Him and hear His heart. The truth is, no one knows what tomorrow holds—and that's okay. In fact, we're not meant to. There's something so much bigger going on than our human desire to control our circumstances and make life less challenging for ourselves. God is creating an infinitely greater picture—one that we can only see a tiny part of right now. And the more we understand and embody this truth, the more peace we will find in letting go and letting Him do His beautiful work within us. You may have a specific reason for holding this book in your hands—maybe you chose it because you're walking through a tough season in life, or maybe someone who cares for you thought it would speak to your heart. No matter how these messages have reached you today, just remember—the truths they contain are timeless. They can be held in your heart for whenever you need them most to bring you comfort and peace in the days and years to come.

Pursue Peace

God's comfort and peace are always available, no matter what circumstances we face. In moments of uncertainty or overwhelming stress, we can take refuge in the truth that He is near. His presence is not dependent on our feelings, nor does it waver when life feels chaotic. Instead, His peace is steadfast, offering rest for our weary hearts and strength for the journey ahead.

Today, ask yourself: Am I trying to carry my burdens on my own? What is the result? Am I anxious, exhausted, or discouraged? How can I surrender my worries to God and trust in His greater plan today?

When we actively pursue God's peace in our lives, He will show up! His peace does not come from perfect circumstances but from knowing that He holds us securely in His hands. No matter where you find yourself today—whether in a season of sorrow, of waiting, or of uncertainty—God's comfort and peace are present and real. He invites you to draw near, lay your burdens at His feet, and receive the rest your soul longs for. His love is unwavering, His grace is sufficient, and His peace is yours to embrace. Take a deep breath, lean into His promises, and know that you are never alone. God's presence goes before you, walks beside you, and surrounds you with a love that will never fail.

Letting Go, Living Free

Surrender to what is. Let go of what was. Have faith in what will be.

SONIA RICOTTI

We all face situations in life that remind us that we aren't in control of anything, really, except our thoughts and actions. Maybe it happens when we step onto an airplane that someone else is flying, or when we've entrusted a sick loved one into the care of a hospital staff, or when we're hoping for a certain outcome, and we just don't know which way it's going to go. Sometimes when there's a lot up in the air, the idea of micromanaging the universe seems quite appealing. Sure, we may trust God to take care of us, but we have some really specific ideas about how He might go about doing that!

It's okay that we have a hard time letting go of expectations. They are simply our best attempts to create the life we think will be best for us. And often, we're just trying to help ourselves feel safe in times of uncertainty. It can be tough to admit that those expectations are made of our very limited understanding of the big picture and of the way God is allowing our lives to unfold in His perfect way and time. But here's an encouraging thought: those up-in-the-air moments can be wonderful (not *easy*, but wonderful) catalysts for our spiritual growth. They are the moments that expand our capacity to trust—the "Be still, and know that I am God" moments (Psalm 46:10 NIV). The ones where we stop overthinking, overplanning, and overworking ourselves to try and make something happen. When we breathe deeply and remember *all will be well because it's all in His hands.* Every last detail.

Pursue Peace

Even when we aren't facing something epic and life-changing, we have small opportunities every day to practice letting go of control, and that builds our spiritual muscles for navigating the bigger things. Next time you're standing in line at a grocery store or coffee shop, frustrated by someone's slow progress, remind yourself that God's timing is perfect. There are reasons you're where you are in this time of your life. You can even look around for how God is working in this season of your life. Maybe the guy behind you needs a reassuring smile. Or the barista in front of you could use some extra grace at the moment. Guess what? You can be the one to offer it! You might be traveling and your rental car deal falls through or you miss your flight. Before scrambling to figure out your next move, stop yourself and take a soul-deep breath. Find reassurance in the truth that God already knew how this would play out and there was a reason He allowed it. Ask for guidance. Trust that He has something better for you down the line.

Growing Good Thoughts

We must cultivate our own garden.
VOLTAIRE

There's something our Creator has given us to care for, like a garden, and the more we tend to it, the more peace and assurance we will live with all day long. That "something" is our minds. And sometimes, these minds of ours are filled with good, true, and beautiful things. But other times, we can experience just the opposite. Let's call it the "snowball effect." Sound familiar? It happens when small worries or concerns are left unattended, start gaining ground, and grow bigger and bigger until they suddenly seem larger than life. Over time, those thoughts take up more and more precious space in our minds that could be filled instead with the good stuff like joy, gratitude, and contentment.

God gave us the potential to live with a vibrant inner landscape, and there are new things growing and blooming within us every day. But He also gave us the job of being caretakers of that landscape. Our minds can't thrive if we don't make the effort to nurture them, which means protecting them from what doesn't belong there and making sure we take in plenty that does. It takes intention and practice to create fertile ground for those life-giving, faith-filled thoughts to take root within us. If we wait until the weeds of doubt and fear have taken over, it may be a lot longer before we can feel deep inner peace again in any lasting way.

Pursue Peace

See if you can get a picture of what's going on within your mind right now. Try asking yourself questions like these: How's life been feeling for me lately? Have I had an underlying sense of peace and trust in God's guidance, even amid my daily challenges? Or have I had a sense of foreboding, dread, or uncertainty in some way? Consider sitting quietly in prayer and asking for any "snowballs" to be revealed that might be causing anxiety and stealing your joy.

Try this: List any persistent thoughts or worries that you feel are weighing you down right now—even those small, nagging ones that just never seem to go away. If there are to-dos that keep calling for your attention, add them to the list, too, and think of a few steps you might take toward resolving them. Make that call you've been putting off, gather some info—whatever small thing you can do to simplify and reduce stress for yourself. Then, acknowledge the things on your list that are out of your control and give them to God. Remember, it's all a process, but each small step you take can remove something negative and create more space within you for things that are positive, and that means greater freedom and joy in your life every day.

Rocking the Boat

Never trade your uniqueness for approval.

JOY MARINO

Our lives are filled with decisions that only we can make. Of course, a lot of those are small ones—what to wear, whom to have coffee with, where to go for a haircut. But sometimes they're bigger decisions—the kind we feel the need to seek God's guidance for. And as we do our best to follow His lead, we're invited to rest in the assurance that we're making the right decisions for us, regardless of the countless opinions of others. This can be especially tough when we're feeling called to blaze a trail in some way—maybe being the first person in our family or inner circle to do something different. It might be a big move, or a new church, or even being honest about something no one else wants to address. There are many ways this can play out in our lives, and it's never easy to be the pioneer. Often, people don't want to deal with someone in their circle of influence making a change. Maybe it brings up something for *them* that they don't want to look at. Maybe they're quite comfortable in their relationship with you, even though it's clear there are some things that need to be brought to light. Maybe watching you follow *your* dreams reminds them that they gave up on *theirs*. But can you imagine what it was like for Jesus—all the people He disappointed and the earthly expectations He did not meet because He chose to listen to One Voice instead of many? It shouldn't surprise us that we, too, may be called to rock the boat in our own way from time to time as we follow Him throughout our lives.

Pursue Peace

Every day there are so many things for us to navigate—decisions, situations, relationships—and we will face them in one of two ways: in fear or in faith. If we put other people's opinions on a pedestal, if we compromise our calling to keep others comfortable, we're acting out of fear. And although God loves and accepts us just as much in our fear as in our faith, He wants more for us. He sees who we can become and how much more joy and purpose we can live with if we are able to trust in His guidance, no matter what others think.

Start noticing the times in your life when you feel swayed by the opinions and influence of others. Remind yourself that those are directions from someone else's compass. And while there may be great wisdom in their advice, you have both the freedom and responsibility to discern God's leading for yourself. Don't ever forget that you have your own inner compass to guide you, provided by your Maker. When you find yourself wondering what to do next, you can always ask Him for direction first. Above all, grant yourself lots of grace. God does! He knows you're doing the best you can to take positive steps in your life, and that's a wonderful direction to be taking!

Connecting with God

Let us pray every day with hearts wide open so that God might meet us in whatever way He chooses.
ANONYMOUS

Prayer is a lifelong conversation with God that's unique to each of us. And especially during tough times, we learn that prayer is so much deeper than an obligation; it can be a haven for our restless spirits, a refreshing place where we can be our truest selves in the presence of the purest love. That's why it's good to remember that the way we pray will likely evolve throughout our lives as we are drawn to connect with God in new ways. And the more open we are to that change, the more authentic our relationship with Him will continue to be.

For example, there are times when we go to pray that we have to admit we just aren't feelin' it. Maybe we're stuck on the hamster wheel of overthinking, or we're tired or discouraged or even (if we're honest) unmotivated at the moment. We know how much we need that sacred connection with God, so we show up hoping that something will click. Yesterday or last week may have been completely different. That's just how it works! Our spiritual connections ebb and flow, just like our human ones do. Of course, we know that God never moves away from us. We just may not sense His presence as strongly on some days. And on those days, we have two choices: we can give up, or we can shake things up! We can try a different way of connecting and see what happens. We can seek out a new experience and look for Him in it, trusting that He knows our hearts and delights in our efforts to draw close to Him.

Pursue Peace

The next time you're having trouble entering into prayer, think about trying something new. What about a change in your environment? How can your senses help you to experience God's presence in a different way? Try playing a song that moves you—whether it makes you get up and dance or brings tears to your eyes and tugs at your heart every time you hear it. Maybe nature is your thing—get outside and feel the grass under your feet, see an endless sky full of billowy clouds or shining stars above you, and let it become a moment of praise. Soak in the warmth of a tub, write a poem, or watch children playing in a park (go down the slide if it brings your heart joy). Make yourself the coldest glass of lemonade on a hot day and savor the tarty sweetness.

God gave us these bodies so that we might experience Him in countless ways on this earth. And while we may *think* we know what's happening in those set-aside times of prayer, sometimes our commitment to meet with Him takes us in new directions. Sometimes He leads us into experiences that are beyond words so we can simply be present with Him. The more we practice simply showing up, the more natural it will become. Even our everyday lives with Him can be a beautiful adventure.

PAUSE FOR PRAYER

Heavenly Father,

In the middle of challenging situations and uncertainty, I come before You seeking Your perfect peace. My heart feels heavy, my mind is restless, and the burdens of life seem to be pressing down upon me. And yet I know that You are my refuge and strength, a very present help in trouble.

Lord, calm my anxious thoughts and fill me with Your presence. Remind me that no storm is too great for Your power, and no sorrow is beyond Your comfort. Help me to trust in Your plans, even when I cannot see the way ahead. Grant me the courage to face each day with faith and the assurance that You are with me.

I ask that Your peace, which passes all understanding, would guard my heart and my mind in Christ Jesus. May Your love be my anchor, and may Your grace sustain me through every challenge I face today.

In Jesus's name, amen.

Loving You

Self-compassion is simply giving the same kindness to ourselves that we would give to others.

DR. CHRISTOPHER GERMER

One way that we experience God's compassion for us is *through* us. It can take a minute for that thought to sink in, and it's difficult to comprehend sometimes! While our heavenly Father calls us to share His love with everyone we meet, we must never forget that we, ourselves, are on that list! Our relationship with ourselves is more important than we may realize. In fact, it's been said that it sets the tone for every other relationship in our lives. What do you think? How much do you enjoy your own company? How often do you remind yourself of those wonderful, God-given qualities you possess? And how often do you find reasons to criticize or devalue yourself? If you're like many people, you know how it feels to be your own best friend *and* your own worst enemy at times.

Often people who are hard on themselves are also critical of others (either vocally or silently). Of course, that's not true of everyone, but when we are heavy on self-judgment, it will usually affect our relationships in one way or another. Our inner world will often be reflected in our outer world, and if we seek to build healthy connections with others, we need to begin within. Ask God to help you—He'll be glad to guide you as you begin.

Pursue Peace

No matter how you feel about yourself today, one thing is undeniably true: you are a unique and beloved creation of God who belongs here on earth, at this time in history. If you feel like you've honored that truth in your life, how wonderful! But if you think maybe that person looking back at you in the mirror could use a little more care, then why not take a few small steps in that direction?

Take a few minutes to prayerfully consider how you feel on a typical day. Do you feel at home in yourself with a sense of peace, or is there a critic lurking, always pointing out your flaws and missteps? Think about the needs you have that aren't being met right now. Are there a few of them that you could start meeting for yourself? Maybe you need more rest, or better boundaries, or a regular grocery store run for healthy stuff so you can stop berating yourself for sneaking junk food!

When we need to feel God's loving care, let's remember the ways He may be calling us to show it to ourselves. There's great comfort and healing to be found in our own hearts as we draw near to Him and allow Him to love us *through* us. That's a gift we can give ourselves at any moment in our lives.

This Is the Day

How we spend our days is, of course, how we spend our lives.
ANNIE DILLARD

Sometimes we miss what God is providing for us in the moment because we're looking right past it. We don't mean to, of course, but we can often be distracted by an ideal future that many of us create in our minds called "someday." Sound familiar? If "someday" were an actual day, it would be jam-packed for a lot of us. We'd be finishing our to-do lists, achieving our most cherished dreams, and doing those things that for years we've been promising ourselves we would do. But there's another day that's infinitely more promising than that one. It's a day that shows up quite often—a day that holds exactly what God knows we need. It is filled with many opportunities and reasons to be grateful. And if we need to get something done, it offers twenty-four hours to choose from. That day is called *today.*

The Bible reminds us of the significance of today in this oft-quoted, well-loved verse: "This is the day that the Lord has made; let us rejoice and be glad in it" (Psalm 118:24 ESV). At some point in adulthood, it may truly hit us how fleeting our time on earth is compared to the eternity that stretches beyond it. And while the gift of heaven is priceless beyond words, there are many specific reasons, large and small, why we are here now. Every morning you wake up to live another one of them, your Maker has plans for you: plans to bless you, lead you, help you grow, and remind you just how near He is—not *someday*, but *this* day.

Pursue Peace

One way to find peace and contentment in our days is to pause once in a while and look at how we're spending them. Of course, no two days will ever be alike. Even if we have a fairly set schedule, life will always bring the unexpected. But if we step back and really look at our daily habits, the motions we go through, and how we tend to connect with others, we might find some things we want to adjust. Maybe we'll discover that some of the time we spend on our screens could be better spent nurturing non-virtual, face-to-face, soul-filling connections. Instead of offering people "should-vitations" *(Hey, we should get together soon!)*, we could follow through and make it happen.

Consider spending some time in prayer reflecting on what makes up your daily life. Maybe write it out on a little note so you can get a good glimpse of the things that tend to fill those precious, twenty-four-hour gifts of time you're given.

Let's ask God to help us make the most of our days so that as we reflect on our lives, we can know that we did all we could with the time we were given.

The Beauty of Perspective

We don't see things as they are, we see them as we are.

ANAÏS NIN

The way we experience our lives today has a lot to do with how we look at them. And if we find ourselves praying for a lighter heart and a calmer spirit, it helps to consider the role we play in receiving what God has to offer. Here's an illustration for you: When you were little, did you ever lie on the grass, look up at passing clouds in the sky, and make up stories about them? We all see something different in the clouds, depending on our unique perspectives. Life is similar to cloud gazing when you think about it. Everything we see and experience will be interpreted by each of us in our own way. Whether an object, an event, or a person's behavior—whatever it is that we witness outside of us is seen through a filter that exists within us.

The Bible reminds us to pay attention to *how we're seeing,* not just *what we're seeing.* If we're quick to judge someone, where is that coming from? Are we looking through the lens of our own opinions and expectations? Or how about when we face a challenge in our lives and we're feeling discouraged? How are we looking at that challenge? Are we automatically expecting the worst, or are we leaving room for possibility? Can we make it a regular practice to look for all the ways God can work in these situations—opening us up to possibility, teaching us something new, and even blessing us unexpectedly? Those passing "clouds" in our lives can take many forms, and we always have the freedom to choose how we will see them.

Pursue Peace

Becoming more aware of the filter we're looking through can help us respond thoughtfully rather than react carelessly to the people and situations in our lives. Try to make it a regular practice in the coming days to notice how your thoughts give meaning to your experiences. Especially when you face a relationship challenge or an unexpected situation, you may discover some familiar patterns in how you interpret things.

Of course, you don't have to try to turn every "lemony" situation into lemonade. Some things are just downright tough to deal with, and some days, we all need the space to feel upset or discouraged for a bit—maybe vent some frustration or have a good cry. We can give ourselves grace for those cloudy thoughts, knowing that God loves us on our grouchy days just as much as on our bright, cheerful days.

One thing we can *always* do, no matter how we feel, is leave room for God to show up. We can take a moment and prayerfully acknowledge both the reality of the situation and the hope we always have in Him: "Lord, this is hard, and I feel discouraged. But I know You are always at work." As long as we keep our eyes on Him, we can trust that everything else will be resolved in due time.

The Gift of Being You

In a world where you can be anything, be yourself.

ETTA TURNER

One way we can experience God's peace more fully in our lives is by living more authentically—being true to who He created us to be. There's an old tale that illustrates this truth beautifully. It's about a mouse who lives in a little cottage in the forest. The mouse spends her days knitting sweaters, chopping firewood, and gathering nuts and berries to store for the winter. She has an instinct to do these things, and she finds great purpose in them. Some of the other forest creatures tease her about being an oddball; they wonder why she doesn't get out more and frolic like they do. But she pays them no mind. Soon, winter comes with blizzards and below-zero temperatures. It's the worst in years, and the animals are unprepared and freezing. They remember the mouse and imagine the warm clothes, blazing fires, and pantry full of food she must have after all that preparation. They knock on her door, and she welcomes them with kindness and provides all they need to survive the winter.

God created each of us with a particular mix of abilities, desires, and natural tendencies—just like the mouse in the story. These unique traits may have been discovered and nurtured when we were children, or they may have been misunderstood and dismissed. No matter how much we have allowed ourselves to live out who we are, those God-given treasures we carry within us will never go away. He waits patiently for us to discover them and share them with the world. You can never fully comprehend the gift you're giving those around you by simply being yourself.

Pursue Peace

How about you? How aware are you of your gifts, passions, and dreams? Pay close attention to what lights you up and brings joy to your life; consider those abilities that seem to come naturally to you. Is there anything you feel particularly drawn to but aren't sure how to pursue? Take some time in prayer to ask for help discerning the things God may be calling you to. If you ask, you can always trust that He'll make those things clear in His time.

Of course, the more you're operating out of the gifts He has given you and pursuing the dreams He has placed in your heart, the more satisfying your life will be. And the more purpose you'll find—just like the little mouse—as doors open that only your Maker could see ahead of time. And here's something else we can all do: support others on their journeys, no matter how unusual their lives seem to us. We can remember how vastly different God's plan can look in every life and encourage one another to pursue whatever way He leads.

A Time to Rest

When you rest, you catch your breath, and it fills your lungs and holds you up, like water wings.
ANNE LAMOTT

"And on the seventh day God ended His work which He had done, and He rested" (Genesis 2:2 NKJV). We sometimes hear this Bible verse referenced when people talk about feeling depleted. It's hard to deny the importance of setting aside time in our lives to reflect and recharge. It takes humility to admit that we can't do everything all the time! We were created with a need to pause, and our physical and mental health will suffer if we ignore that need for too long.

So, how are you finding peace in rest these days? What does "rest" look like to you? We each have our own answer to that question, and it's always changing, depending on what season of life we are in. That's why it's so important for us to tune in regularly to ourselves and listen to what our minds and bodies are truly calling for when it comes to downshifting. It may be as simple as committing to eight hours of sleep for a while (which can be a challenge for those of us who often burn the candle at both ends). It may mean setting aside some time to sit outdoors in our favorite beautiful spot or designating a family day that's all about relaxing together without an agenda. It could be many different things over the years, depending on circumstances and life stages, but one thing it can *always* be is a priority in our lives. Rest is one of those gifts we give ourselves that will benefit us for a lifetime.

Pursue Peace

Think about the balance you experience in your daily life. Are you on the go most of the time? Do you feel like you have room to breathe—a margin of downtime that allows you to recharge when you need to? If not, do you think you could find a few places on your calendar to pencil in a small, regular window of intentional rest? Maybe it's setting aside a half hour of quiet time just a few days a week and making the promise to stick to it—like a date you keep with yourself. Or it could look like a few nights of committing to getting just one extra hour of sleep.

Even the smallest step can add up to a big change in your sense of well-being. Plus, making a commitment to yourself and keeping it reminds you that you are so worth taking care of—and your Creator backs that up 100 percent! "And the very hairs on your head are all numbered. . . . You are more valuable to God than a whole flock of sparrows" (Luke 12:7 NLT). Finding rest may involve asking for a little help from a spouse, friend, or family member. But always remember that you'd happily do the same to support them in caring for themselves (and you probably have).

PAUSE FOR PRAYER

Dear Jesus,

Thank You so much for the precious gift of Your peace—a peace I can't even begin to understand with my human mind. Thank You that Your peace guards my heart, no matter what I face in this uncertain world each day. You are my constant, my refuge, my Source of unshakable calm. Even when the challenges of my day threaten to overwhelm me, I know You are near—I am never alone, and I can always call on You for help!

Lord, I am so grateful that the peace You give me doesn't depend on what I'm going through; it's rooted in Your unfailing love and Your sovereign plan for my life. You guide my steps, calm my fears, and remind me that I can trust You completely. When worry tries to creep into my thoughts, Your peace speaks louder, calling me back to rest in You.

Thank You for walking with me through every season of my life, leading me with wisdom and grace. Help me to keep my heart anchored in Your truth and share Your peace with those around me. May my life reflect the assurance that comes from knowing You are in control!

In Your precious name, amen.

Unexpected Outcomes

Faith means believing in advance what will only make sense in reverse.
PHILIP YANCEY

Let this truth find its way to your heart, and remind yourself of it often: you can trust God with every detail of your life, even when you don't quite understand what He's up to. Things may not (and probably won't) unfold exactly as you expect, but He will *never* let you down.

Have you ever hoped and prayed for something so much and had a strong feeling it was going to work out? Maybe you asked for guidance and saw signs that seemed to point you toward a particular path. Or you heard a great message that lined up perfectly with your plan. You felt hopeful and certain, but then, for whatever reason, things went in a different direction. Maybe you wondered: *How did I miss it? What did I do wrong?* . . . and most significantly: *What happens next time? Will I be afraid to step out in faith again?* Times like these can leave us feeling discouraged and disappointed. But they can also do something unexpectedly wonderful for us: they can draw us closer to God if we are willing to bring our hurting hearts to Him. We can be completely honest with Him about how we're feeling—disappointed, confused, frustrated. And in that honesty, our connection with Him is strengthened. That's how relationships work, right? The more we communicate, the closer we become. And sometimes, it's the tough things in life that create the deepest connections.

Pursue Peace

Here's one thing you may have heard about prayers: *they're always answered, just not always how we expect.* Next time you're feeling disheartened about an unanswered prayer, instead of allowing a cloud of discouragement to settle in, why not use it as an opportunity to really dig in and draw close to God? He wants nothing more than for us to seek His heart in every circumstance. Ask everything you can think to ask! *Why did it happen this way? What am I supposed to see in this? How can it teach me more about myself and about You?*

The next time you need to step out in faith—even if uncertainty creeps in—remind yourself that it's safe to step out boldly with confidence because God knows exactly what's up. Just go in the direction you're led, and know that no matter how hard you knock, He will only open doors that are best for you to walk through, and He'll close the ones that aren't.

Most importantly, in the process, you'll learn more about Him and about who He's created you to be. And that's what this faith journey is all about.

Serving God Alone

It is amazing what you can accomplish if you do not care who gets the credit.
HARRY S. TRUMAN

Sometimes God invites us to look within ourselves for what we've been depending on others to provide. This is especially true when it comes to being recognized or appreciated for something we've done. Whether we've achieved a small act of service or a significant accomplishment, receiving a pat on the back or an expression of gratitude can be wonderful—an encouraging reminder that our efforts haven't gone unnoticed. But there are times in our lives (parenthood, volunteering, or even our jobs outside our homes) when we work hard to provide something and there's no fanfare involved—maybe not even a "Thank you!" or "Great job!" to be heard. As discouraging as these times can be, they can also be blessings in disguise. How? They point us toward the One who *does* see and appreciate every little effort we make in our lives—every sacrifice, every late night, every early morning we give, and every goal we painstakingly achieve. Our heavenly Father delights in the good things we do, just as we delight in seeing the children in our lives learn to serve others and accomplish new things. However, if those children grow up forever looking for someone else to validate their efforts, they'll live with a lot of disappointment. They need to learn to appreciate themselves, even when no one else is watching. And there's a gift we can give them that God provides for all of us—the ability to celebrate our own growth and recognize our own accomplishments, regardless of who else notices. We can experience joy in the fact that the One who matters most sees it all.

Pursue Peace

Here's something to try in the coming days: do a few things on purpose that you know you won't be recognized for. It could be as simple as taking a loop on the walking trail in your neighborhood to pick up trash or paying for the person behind you in the drive-through. It could be setting a personal goal for yourself that you've been wanting to accomplish and then celebrating it quietly when you achieve it. Maybe have a little one-person "woo-hoo" moment! Turn up some music loud and dance for the joy of it, or treat yourself to that over-the-top, decadent coffee drink and savor every sip. Feel the sense of confidence you're building within, and soak in the satisfaction of a job well done.

Letting our personal experience of something be enough, without having to post about it on social media or have others notice it, is a good practice for all of us. Our heavenly Father cares deeply about our growth and surely takes great joy in our accomplishments. He will always be our audience of One. So, next time you do something worthy of a pat on the back and find yourself waiting for one, reach right back there and do it yourself. Thank Him for being present in every detail of your life, and enjoy that moment of recognition within.

Your Own Pace

Transformation is a process . . . a journey of discovery.

RICK WARREN

I would bet that you've heard a butterfly metaphor or two in your time—and for good reason! Many of us needing hope and reassurance in our lives have been inspired by the miraculous metamorphosis that takes place in nature—from caterpillar to cocoon and beyond. You may also have heard about how the body of that caterpillar breaks down to almost nothing before being reorganized into the winged wonder that emerges. God's creation is amazing!

And while the same kind of thing happens on our faith journeys, we can sometimes forget how gradual it can be. The incredible change that occurs for the cocooned creature in a few weeks is actually the journey of a lifetime for us. When we make the decision to follow Jesus, there's usually not a sudden moment when we can exclaim, "Ta-da! Check out the brand-new me!" Transformation occurs one day at a time for the rest of our lives. But we also have the gift of witnessing the ways God shows up in our lives every day—helping us grow, shedding light on the things we need to let go of for our freedom, and turning our raw material, bit by bit, into something we never imagined possible. It's so important that we remember this process takes time, especially when we find ourselves discouraged about falling back into some of the same old patterns that we thought we'd moved past for good. Whatever He allows us to face again could be for our further healing. If something keeps coming up, that could be God's way of saying, "It's okay—just pay attention. We're still transforming this."

Pursue Peace

Sometimes on these transformation journeys of ours, we run into the "shoulds." Have you ever heard of them? They're demeaning, persistent thoughts that like to remind us of all we haven't yet become. They tell us who we *should* be and what we *should* be doing and how we *should* have parts of our lives put together by now! One powerful thing that we can do to help ourselves stay strong is to fill our hearts with the encouragement found in God's Word. Then, when the "shoulds" do come calling, and we feel that familiar pull toward discouragement, we can resist it. We can have a kind of arsenal of eternal truth to protect us from temporary doubt. Consider gathering promises from the Bible that focus on your transformation in Christ. In II Corinthians 4:16 (NIV), Paul reminds us to "not lose heart" because "inwardly we are being renewed day by day." You could create an affirming reminder or two to speak with confidence during times of self-doubt: "My life is unfolding beautifully in God's time, in God's way." Remember, it's not about being where we *should* be; it's about being where He's brought us today. And tomorrow we can trust that He'll lead us a little further on.

Taking Care of You

Burnout is what happens when you try to avoid being human for too long.
MICHAEL GUNGOR

Self-care chatter is everywhere these days, and maybe that's because we need it more than ever in a world that seems to move at lightning speed. Caring for our minds and bodies requires intention, and when we find ourselves feeling overwhelmed or discouraged in some way, it's good to consider how well we've been caring for ourselves and how much it can affect our overall sense of well-being. Burnout is a real thing, after all, and most of us have experienced it to some degree in our lives. Sometimes it creeps up and hits us out of nowhere; other times, it shows up slowly and gradually. It may be the result of a demanding career, a strenuous season of parenthood, saying yes to too many opportunities, or just being hit with a lot of things at once. Many of us feel it to the extreme. We reach a breaking point, drop into a chair somewhere, and think, *I just can't do this anymore.*

Those can be some of life's toughest moments because of how completely tapped out and powerless we feel. But they can *also* be the most hopeful points of our journeys because it is often at the end of our rope that we experience His presence most profoundly. If you find yourself feeling this kind of soul-deep weariness (or even feeling momentarily overwhelmed), remember that it will pass. We're sometimes allowed to reach those breaking points so we can truly grasp the importance of caring for these bodies, minds, and hearts that God has given us . . . and so we can remember that our true sustenance will always be found in Him.

Pursue Peace

When we *do* start to feel overwhelmed, instead of ignoring it and just hoping it'll pass, we can take the time to pay attention to where it might be coming from. It could simply be that we have too much on our plates! If this happens to you, consider looking at all you're trying to accomplish and see where you might let a few things go—or at least cut them in half. Does *all* the laundry need to be done right now? Can you ask someone else to pick up the kids today? Can you just be honest and say, "I need to reschedule this coffee date because I'm exhausted, and I'd rather connect with you when I can be my best self"?

There are small things we can do for ourselves every day to help maintain balance in our lives and avoid heading toward burnout. We can start by making sure we're incorporating plenty of self-care—whether that be scheduling naps, taking walks, or promising ourselves a relaxing bath at the end of the day. We can make it a regular practice to pause before saying yes to a new opportunity. Often, a simple "Can I let you know tomorrow?" or "I need to pray about that" is all we need to ensure that we're listening to our gut and God's guidance.

Let Them Shine

There are two ways of spreading light:
to be the candle or the mirror that reflects it.
EDITH WHARTON

Some of us have had the lyrics to the song "This Little Light of Mine" memorized since our earliest childhood years. Others learned later in life that Jesus is the Light of the World and that we are all called to reflect His light. Regardless, we got the gist of it at some point—we're called to open our hearts and allow Him to shine through us in ways that we could never muster on our own. Of course, this involves finding opportunities to share His love and to use the gifts God has given us to bless the people around us. It also means helping *others* find ways to shine. And in the world today, we may know a few people in our communities whose light has dimmed a bit. It's possible they've been in survival mode in some way, and we may know from experience that when that happens, we humans often don't have much energy to look outward. In fact, they may seem downright self-centered. But the truth is, they're just trying to do whatever they can to hold it together.

There are also folks in our lives right now who just haven't found a way to let the light come through. They may feel the desire to reach out, connect, and make a difference in some way, but they have no idea where to start. Helping people to share their light can be one of the most rewarding experiences on our faith journey. It's a little taste of God's kingdom—living as we're meant to live, helping one another find the fullest expressions of our lives in Him.

Pursue Peace

Sometimes we shine the brightest for God when we help someone else to uncover their light. It's not about trying to fix them or point out their missed opportunities. It is about encouraging them, reminding them of their unique gifts, and inviting them to open their hearts to new possibilities. If you feel drawn to encourage someone, ask God for the best timing. Ask Him to give you the words they most need to hear to inspire them—not just the words you think they need. Ask for courage to speak the truth in love.

If this isn't something you've even thought about before, you're not alone! Many of us are so busy just figuring out how to walk our own path that we haven't noticed that someone beside us may have hidden their lamp under a basket (see Matthew 5:15). So, take a look around at the light you see coming from others. Do you notice potential in someone who may just need a little nudge or vote of confidence? Many people simply need to be reminded of the gifts God has given them to bless the world in their unique ways. Let's make it a point to lift someone up today and help them along the path to discovering all they're created to be.

PAUSE FOR PRAYER

Dear Lord Jesus,

Thank You for the precious gift of the Holy Spirit, who fills our hearts with peace beyond our understanding. You promised that we would never be alone, and through Your Spirit, we are constantly surrounded by Your presence, love, and guidance. In moments of uncertainty, fear, and stress, the Holy Spirit whispers truth to our hearts, reminding us that You are near and that we can trust in Your perfect plan.

Lord, I am so grateful that Your peace is not based on my circumstances but on the unshakable foundation of Your love. When life seems overwhelming, Your Spirit brings calm to my soul. When anxiety threatens to creep in, You remind me to rest in You. Teach me to walk daily in the peace that comes from abiding in Your presence. Help me to surrender my worries and trust fully in Your goodness and Your good plan for my life.

Jesus, I ask that You would fill my heart with more of Your peace. Let it overflow into my thoughts, my words, and my actions so that I may be a vessel of Your peace to others.

In Your wonderful name I pray.

Amen.

Grateful for What Is

The grass is greener where you water it.

NEIL BARRINGHAM

Gratitude is like a balm for our spirits. It can bring us deep satisfaction in our lives, regardless of our circumstances. It transfers our focus from what we *don't* have to what we *do* have. Gratitude is a little shift that our hearts can make anytime toward God's goodness—a little shift that can make a big difference. And that's extra important for us to remember when we're dealing with a struggle that no one likes to face: *envy.*

Envy is something we all encounter at times in life. We may try to hide it. Ignore it. Beat ourselves up for feeling it. And even wonder, *Good grief. Why can't I see that the grass is just as green over here?* The grass will always be greenest where we water it!

How do we water our grass and appreciate God's blessings in our lives? With our praise. We take a good look at what we do have in our lives, and we find ways to say, "Thank You." *Thank You, Lord, for this blessing. This job. This opportunity. This home that may be small or messy, but it's still my home. This body that may be imperfect, but it's the one You gave me, and I'm doing the best I can to care for it.* The more we take our eyes off what others possess (which can be tough these days when it's coming at us from everywhere), the more we can find contentment, right where we are, with what we have.

Pursue Peace

One thing that doesn't help when we find ourselves feeling discontented, ungrateful, or just downright frustrated about what's missing in our lives is to beat ourselves up for feeling that way. Remember, ungratefulness and envy try to creep in on all of us! But the good news is once we become aware that we're headed down the path of jealousy or ingratitude, we can start taking steps in a more positive direction. Here are a few ideas to help:

Be creative: Sit down with your journal, reflect on your life, and challenge yourself to make a list of blessings you've never considered before. Then, take a moment to thank God for those things.

Flip the script: Try a completely different approach if it feels right to you! If there is a certain someone in your life who seems to trigger you in this area, try moving *toward* them instead of away. Find ways to genuinely appreciate this person as a unique creation of God. Maybe even commit to praying for this person in the coming days. Chances are, once you shift gears, you'll recognize that they are just as human as you are and have just as many struggles as strengths.

Is Anyone Listening?

Listening is about being present, not just about being quiet.

KRISTA TIPPETT

These days, when words seem plentiful, silence can be precious and rare. As our phones light up with messages and the internet buzzes with new content, finding some quiet for our minds and hearts can feel like a true respite—especially when we're dealing with tough things in our lives. In fact, sometimes what we really need is someone to sit with us in that silence and hear our hearts. What a gift the presence of a true listener can be—not someone who's waiting for their turn to talk, or coming up with ideas to fix us, or even thinking up some verses to inspire us. *Of course,* it's wonderful to be on the receiving end of encouragement. But some moments simply call for a loving friend to be with us in our struggles.

James 1:19 (NIV) reminds us to be "quick to listen" and "slow to speak." The people in our lives who can do both are true blessings. If we don't have any supportive listeners in our lives, it's never too late to ask God to bring someone along. And we, in turn, can be that kind of support for others. When someone comes to us with a problem and needs to vent or just tell their story, we can practice the patience of truly listening. If we're in the habit of searching for solutions or trying to help fix things as quickly as possible, we can try something different: we can take a breath, take in everything they're saying, and allow them the space to feel it before we respond. Those moments of silence may clear the way for God to speak to both of our hearts.

Pursue Peace

You can learn a lot about yourself by paying close attention to your conversations with others. Do you feel like there's a good balance in your exchanges, or do you often get the sense that you're not really being heard? Do you wish you had more intentional listeners in your life?

If you don't feel you have good listeners in your inner circle, ask God to help you share that need with those who love you. You might also consider investing in more connections with people who can provide some patient, quiet encouragement when you need it. As most of us have experienced, a few intentional words spoken at the right time can be much more effective than an outpouring of well-meaning but careless words of advice.

And on the flipside, think about how you show up for others. Pay attention to your conversations in the days to come and see what your natural tendencies are. Do you form an answer before others finish talking? Are you comfortable allowing a pause, or do you feel the need to fill it up with words? If you don't like what you observe, then take some small steps toward change. Be intentional about listening. Allow more space and see how God might work through you in the in-between.

Freedom from Fear

On the other side of fear lies freedom.

ANONYMOUS

We never outgrow the need for reassurance in our lives, especially when it comes to finding the courage to step out of our comfort zones. Life can bring some daunting challenges, but those challenges can be blessings in disguise. They can lead us through the forest of our fears and allow us to emerge on the other side with greater strength and confidence. It feels wonderful to look back and exclaim, "Wow, I really did it!" But as most of us have discovered, the journey from A to B isn't easy.

The words *courage* and *encouragement* share the same core idea—*developing from the heart* (the Latin word is *cor*). The heart is where every brave action begins. If we're open to it, that's where God will meet us in those times we feel most fearful, holding out His hand for us to take as we set out on shaky legs. Sure, we can build ourselves up—gathering all the facts, repeating affirmations, practicing incessantly, and promising ourselves great rewards for our bravery—but real courage will always start with Him working in our hearts. We can discover an indomitable spirit right at the center of who we are, inspired by Jesus's words: "With God all things are possible" (Matthew 19:26 NIV). Even if you're not facing something epic at this moment, most days offer little opportunities to move forward in faith when you feel like retreating in fear, whether it's a conversation you've been putting off, an idea you've been reluctant to share, or a step you've been wanting to take toward something bigger. You're always invited to visit the quiet center within, where God's reassuring presence dwells to nudge you lovingly onward.

Pursue Peace

Fear is so personal to each of us. What takes one person every ounce of courage they can muster may be a walk in the park for another. It's easy to look at something that someone else is facing and wonder why it seems to be such a big deal to them. But we can be hard on ourselves sometimes too—wondering why we can't just take a leap of faith. Nobody else seems to be incessantly worried about their parachute opening—what's wrong with us? It helps to remember that we're never comparing apples to apples. As God's unique creations, we will always have different struggles and strengths. We're just wonderfully diverse like that!

Whether or not we're facing something big at the moment, we can always build our faith muscles by reminding ourselves often of the strong foundation we stand on. We can have phrases of truth that reflect God's promises ready for moments of hesitation: *The peace of Christ is with me* (John 20:21); *God will strengthen, help, and hold me* (Isaiah 41:10); *I trust in Jesus* (John 14:1); *He delivers me from all my fears* (Psalm 34:4). Remember, when you start to move into fear, you can take a soul-deep breath and return to your calm center where the Holy Spirit wants to assure you that you have all you need within.

Building Bridges

Compassion opens limitless doors to human connection.

STEVE GILLILAND

We live in a time that can feel scary and uncertain for a lot of us because of the dissonance and division we witness around us. We're bombarded with an "us versus them" mentality. *Follow this person, not that one. Believe my story, not theirs.* It can make us feel like strangers to each other, when really, we all carry the same deep need inside—the need to feel safe, connected, and loved just as we are.

About two thousand years ago, Jesus entered a world that had divided itself in many ways—culturally, religiously, and politically—all things we humans still deal with today. But despite what people expected Him to do, He did quite the opposite. He didn't set out to conquer and declare the superiority of one tribe or type of person over another. He had a completely different intention, and that was to bring the love of the Father to everyone. He reached across divides, welcomed those who had been rejected, and spoke the painful truth to the ones who'd always mistakenly believed that they were better than the rest. When we consider how we might follow Him today—bringing God's peace into the midst of division—Christ's example can be a wonderful place to start. We can step right into the crossfire of all the differing beliefs, opinions, judgments, and agendas and go straight to radically loving everyone. When we find ourselves feeling fearful or uncertain about what's happening around us, let's remember the power of what lies within us: the unconditional love of Christ for every person on the planet.

Pursue Peace

We can do many things in our everyday lives to build bridges, and while they may seem simple, they can be powerful—especially when we're following God's lead. When we make ourselves available to carry His love into the world, there's no telling what He'll do through us. Maybe we'll choose to listen to someone, even if we don't agree with their beliefs, just so they can have the chance to be heard. Maybe we'll cross cultural barriers to offer compassion to people whose lives look nothing like ours. Maybe we'll find the courage to shine a light on the unjust actions that divide people.

What are some ways you might feel called to connect with others today? Spending some quiet time in God's presence, just listening to what comes to you, is a wonderful start. Also, start paying close attention to the people you cross paths with—whether online or in the real world. Keep an open heart and listen for God's "still small voice" (I Kings 19:12 KJV) within that may prompt you to reach out to someone. Our heavenly Father knows the intentions of our hearts and will always take what we offer and make something beautiful out of it. We need only to consider the life of Jesus to see what wonderful things can happen when we live as vessels of His love.

Inhale, Exhale

Deep breaths are like little love notes to your body.

ANONYMOUS

There's a reason the age-old advice "Take a deep breath" is still around. It works! When we're trying to find peace in times of stress, a simple inhale and exhale can make a big difference. The funny thing is that we're so used to breathing, we're usually not even aware that it's happening!

If you ever want to know what's really going on in your body, try checking in with your breath. This in-and-out flow of life has accompanied you through every moment of your existence. It's like a gauge that can give you a glimpse of your inner workings at any moment. When you're stressed, your breath is probably shallow. When you're relaxed or in awe of something, it's probably long and deep. When you're afraid, it may be held in altogether! And because it's so interconnected with every part of us, our breath can be a huge help when it comes to calming ourselves in tough times. The Bible makes many mentions of God's breath as a life force and our own breath as a gift from Him to sustain us on the earth. And we can celebrate that gift by using it to its full potential! As we spend time in prayer (which is like breathing for our spirits), we can tend to our physical selves, too, by slowing our breath and allowing it to bring stillness to our minds and bodies.

Pursue Peace

Whether you took an anatomy class in school, work in healthcare, or have just observed the fascinating workings of the human body in some way, it's hard to deny that there's a Creator who orchestrated it all. And our Creator knows exactly what you need to keep your body running well. In the next 365 days, for example, you will take over eight million breaths. While most of them will happen without your awareness, you can always harness the power of those miraculous gifts to use to your advantage!

Consider this: when we encounter a stressful situation, we're often triggered to reach for certain things we've adopted over time to deal with that stress. These things have likely become habits, and for many of us, the habits can be unhealthy. Not only that—they often provide just a few minutes of relief, and then we're right back to where we started, feeling tense and overwhelmed. But deep breathing can have a much healthier, longer-lasting effect. And, in some cases, the effects can be felt immediately.

When we look to God for comfort and peace in stressful times, let's always remember that He has designed us with a wonderful way to help calm ourselves. Even slowing down for a deep inhale and exhale once in a while can contribute to a much calmer spirit over time.

PAUSE FOR PRAYER

Heavenly Father,

You are our Source of true and lasting peace—the only true Source of peace in this world. I come to You today in this world of difficulties and challenges, asking for Your peace to fill both my own heart and the hearts of my children, my family members, and my loved ones. When anxiety or fear tries to take hold of us, please remind each of us that You are always in control and that we can rest in Your perfect love.

Lord, guard our hearts and minds, keeping us steadfast in our faith in You and free from stressing over the big or the little things in our lives. Surround my children and my other loved ones with Your tangible presence, guiding them with Your wisdom and calming any fear they may be experiencing. May they grow in the assurance that You are always with them, leading them in truth and love.

Let your peace flow through all of our lives—through our homes, our relationships, our day-to-day interactions with one another. Help us to trust in You more deeply and then turn around and be a source of peace and comfort to those we encounter.

In Jesus's name, amen.

Dear Me, Lighten Up . . .

And now that you don't have to be perfect, you can be good.
JOHN STEINBECK

Here's an assignment for you today: *go easy on yourself.* Does that sound wonderful or impossible? (Or maybe a little of both?) The truth is, most of us need that reminder quite often in our lives because—drum roll, please—we're human! In fact, you don't have to get far in the Bible (once people show up on the scene) to witness a good amount of imperfection. Mistakes are made, marks are missed, and some pretty devious stuff goes down! And just like our long line of ancestors, we, too, often find ourselves falling short in our own ways—even unintentionally—even when we've tried earnestly to make changes and do better.

Once we open our eyes in the morning, it's likely that at some point during the day, we will have an imperfect moment (or several). Knowing that doesn't have to discourage us though; in fact, the more honest we are with ourselves and others about our realness, the more freedom we have to lighten up and enjoy life. It's not that we tell ourselves to ditch our standards and do whatever we want; it's just that we give ourselves permission to be human in an imperfect world while we do our best to follow Jesus. And most importantly, we remember that the God who made us sees our hearts and knows we're doing the best we can. Instead of berating us for tripping in the first place, He encourages us to dust ourselves off, get back up, and keep trying. Just do the next right thing: take one more step with Him on the journey.

Pursue Peace

One way to find grace for ourselves when we stumble is to imagine what we might say to someone we love if they were to make the same kind of misstep. It's likely we would have much more compassion for them than we do for ourselves in those moments. We might remind them of all the wonderful, positive things about themselves that they're forgetting because they're focusing so much on the negative. We might gently nudge them to pray to their loving Father, who always waits with open arms of forgiveness, comfort, and reassurance.

Here's a healing exercise: think about what you might say in a note to that person you love when they're feeling unworthy, and then take a moment and write a note like that to yourself. Maybe you haven't experienced an epic blunder in a while. Good for you! But maybe there are everyday things in your life that weigh on you—things that you feel aren't good enough or ways you struggle with perfectionism that steal your joy. Speak to yourself with tenderness and understanding, and then read out loud what you wrote and take it in. You might be surprised about the transformation that can happen, little by little, as you focus less on your imperfections and more on God's goodness and grace every day.

The Power to Choose

I don't know what the future may hold, but I know Who holds the future.
RALPH ABERNATHY

Close your eyes for a moment, take a deep breath, and tell yourself this beautiful truth: *all will be well.* Isn't that a wonderful reminder amid life's uncertainty? Most of us could benefit from hearing those words daily! However, we have these other two words that tend to show up in our minds every now and then: *What if?* And the thoughts that follow those words can have a significant effect on our well-being. For many of us, those thoughts tend to be fearful: *What if this doesn't go well? What if I'm not safe? What if she never returns? What if he tells everyone? What if . . . ?* Our God-given imaginations can be used for wonderful things, but when we allow them to be taken over by fear, it casts a shadow in our lives that God didn't intend to be there. We all deal with negative expectations in our lives to some degree and for different reasons. Some of us are afraid to get our hopes up. Others have had unexpected things happen in the past and think that by preparing themselves they won't be blindsided in the future. For whatever reason, as humans, we sometimes take the darker path in our minds. But another part of being human is our ability to choose our thoughts. We just need to be intentional about it: *What if it's not as bad as I think? What if I'll be okay, no matter the outcome?* Sometimes it's simply about remembering that we have a loving Creator who gave us the power to choose and is always there, desiring to help us use our imaginations for good.

Pursue Peace

Are you up for a little *what-if* challenge? When those fears come to mind, start noticing the path that your thoughts naturally take. See if you can move the needle more toward expecting the best instead of the worst. Here's what you need to remember more than anything: the most peaceful path you can ever take toward an unknown future is the one where you walk hand in hand with God. The more you learn to trust Him to lovingly provide for you today, the less you will worry about what tomorrow might bring.

Consider making a list of all the *what-ifs* that tend to weigh you down. Interview yourself about what you're truly afraid of in times of uncertainty. What are those core fears you arrive at routinely, and where did they begin? Ask for God's healing in those areas. Then, make a nice, long list of the positive *what-ifs* you'd like to choose when fear comes knocking.

Be encouraged to know that there will likely be plenty of outcomes in your life that are far more wonderful than you can imagine. And when they aren't, you have a loving Father who knows exactly what you need to see you through.

Whom Do You See?

Our identity rests in God's relentless tenderness for us revealed in Jesus Christ.
BRENNAN MANNING

No matter how you see yourself today, please remember this one precious thing: *you are, at your core, a child of God.* Nothing else about you will ever be more important or more beautiful about you than that truth. You see, every day of our lives we catch glimpses of ourselves in many different mirrors—reflections that tell us who we are. Most of these mirrors aren't hanging on walls. They're a different kind of mirror altogether. They're the people in our lives who look back at us and reflect who we are in their eyes. For instance, children reflect the fact that we are much-needed caretakers; neighbors reflect the truth that our actions affect those around us because we're all connected; our bosses and coworkers reflect our responsibility to do honest work and provide for ourselves and our families. All these connections show us different facets of who we are, and together they help to make up the way we see our place in the world. Relationships help us to learn who we are and how much we matter to the people we're connected with every day. But while these reflections can be powerful reminders of our worth, it's vital for us to remember that they do not *create* our worth and identity. Our identity is found in God alone. Our relationship with Him is the only "mirror" that reflects who we are 100 percent of the time—the clearest "mirror" of our identity and worth that we can look into every day. The more we see ourselves in Him, as His children, the less we depend on others to show us who we are.

Pursue Peace

Whether we interact daily with many people or just a few, whether we work on the road, in an office, or in a piled-high laundry room, we'll always see our reflection in the world around us somehow. It's just the nature of being alive here on planet Earth with the other seven billion or so souls who inhabit it at the moment!

The good news is that we get to choose how we will react to the "mirrors" that our relationships show us. The more firmly rooted we are in God's unconditional love for us, the more our identity is set. Any other facets of ourselves that we see—as workers, creators, parents, spouses, friends, neighbors, or teachers (you get the idea)—are just *parts of* who we are, never the whole.

Pay attention to your different social roles in the next few days and notice how they help make up the way you see yourself. Where do you tend to lean most heavily to find your identity? Consider making a "mirror list" of the many things God says about you as His child. The more you focus on those unchanging aspects of yourself, the more naturally you will lean into them when you start to forget the beautiful truth of who—and Whose—you really are.

At Home in You

Always remember, your body is sacred.
It's the only home God has given you to live in all your life.
ANONYMOUS

This is an invitation to come home to one of the most beautiful places God has provided for you in this life—*your body.* Some of us need that invitation daily because we spend a lot of time in our heads! Consider this: How often do you realize you just did something that you have no recollection of? It could be a small task like washing a dish or starting the coffeemaker. Or it might be something bigger, like the phenomenon called "highway hypnosis," where you've been driving for miles and you suddenly realize you've been so lost in your thoughts that you've driven to your destination without thinking about the directions at all! This kind of checking out is common for most of us in some form or another, and it all has to do with living more in our minds than our bodies.

Regardless of our geographic location, God gave us one unchanging address for this life on earth, and it is the wondrous body we inhabit. Whether you're happy about it or not, the body that is enabling you to sit wherever you're sitting and to read this right now is the only permanent home you'll have in your earthly life. And some of us spend a lot of our days in just one room of that home—our heads. Of course, we're meant to use these minds of ours for many wonderful things. But it's good to check in with ourselves below the neck sometimes, just to see how "at home" we're feeling in the rest of our bodies!

Pursue Peace

Trying to live with more awareness in such a fast-paced, plugged-in world can feel like swimming upstream sometimes. But if we desire a deeper sense of God's presence, then we need to find ways to become more mindful—more present in ourselves and in the moment.

Why not start today, right where you are? Set this book down—maybe even lie down for a few minutes—and take the slowest, deepest breath you can. Feel yourself come back fully to your body. Start from the top of your head and work your way slowly down to your toes, becoming aware of every little part on the way and tuning in to how each part truly feels in this moment. You can even say a prayer of gratitude, thanking your Creator for all that makes you, *you*!

Remember, God knows the particular reasons that you find yourself in your head sometimes, and He also knows how to help you return to the present. If you're feeling like you could use more of that, why not ask Him about it? He may whisper something to your heart through His Word that you hadn't thought of before, or provide a bit of wisdom through someone you know. Your job is simply to pay attention, be open to guidance, and trust that He will always know how to lead you home.

The Road Ahead

Challenges are what make life interesting,
and overcoming them is what makes life meaningful.
JOSHUA MARINE

Drawing close to God as we navigate life's challenges may not make the road smoother, but it will always help us to face what's in front of us with more hope, peace, and purpose. Here's a little illustration: Imagine a road that's in dire need of repair. Let's say this road runs through a neighborhood and many people take it each day. It's full of potholes, and as you watch the traffic drive over it, you see lots of swerving happening—frustrated drivers trying to navigate the obstacles without causing damage to their cars. There are three kinds of people you might find driving through that neighborhood: (1) Those who complain every day about the road conditions. They wonder, *When will someone finally do something?* (2) Those who just plow through and do their best to ignore it. After all, ignorance is bliss—*right?* (3) Those who decide to take some action. They call the transportation department with their concerns, trusting that they'll receive assistance.

These are the ways that many of us approach life's challenges. Some of us are frustrated with the way things are and ask why a lot. Other people just don't want to acknowledge the things that clearly need to be addressed. Finally, there are those who are ready to face those obstacles head-on and make changes. We've learned that complaining just brings us down, and denying doesn't make anything go away. So, we decide to call for help this time around—to lean into God and let Him lead us through.

Pursue Peace

Notice the way different people around you respond to life's challenges. They can often be mirrors for us, showing us what is hard to see in ourselves. We may find ourselves doing the same thing in the future, and we can remember that it isn't how we want to respond.

On the flipside, when we admire someone's ability to navigate the tough stuff with strength and grace, we can make a note of that too! In fact, if there's someone in your life who seems to walk closely with God through difficulty, consider calling them or making a coffee date with them. Ask about their life and how they've learned to lean on Him. It's likely been quite a process, and they probably have some great wisdom to share. You never know when that kind of wisdom will come in handy.

Most importantly, our Maker sees our challenges coming way before we do. He already knows how He's going to use the potholes in our lives for our good—to help us grow and even bless us in ways we can't imagine. His Word is full of promises to provide everything we need on the journey, and the more we fill our hearts with those promises today, the greater our peace will be in the midst of whatever we face tomorrow.

PAUSE FOR PRAYER

Dear Heavenly Father,

When I have to make a difficult decision and I am unsure of what to do, please remind me that I can always come to You, seeking Your divine wisdom and peace. You are the Good Shepherd, who leads His people with love and purpose, and I trust that You will always guide my steps as I seek Your will for my life. When the path ahead feels unclear, remind me that You are always working for my good, even when I cannot see the full picture.

Father, I ask for the assurance of Your Spirit's presence as I make choices that impact my life and the lives of those around me. Quiet my anxious thoughts and replace them with confidence in Your perfect plan. Help me to surrender my fears and lean into Your wisdom, knowing that You are always faithful to direct my steps when I commit to follow You in obedience. Thank You for the peace that follows me when I follow Your will.

May that peace continue to guard my heart as I wait for clarity, and may I trust that wherever You lead, it is for my best. Let my decisions always bring glory to You and draw me closer to Your will and purpose for my life.

In Jesus's name, amen.

All That You Are

There's nothing more inspiring than the complexity and beauty of the human heart.
CYNTHIA HAND

Do you ever get down on yourself about something you're struggling with and can't seem to overcome? If so, think about this: Your life is not made of only one ingredient. You are a whole person, full of beautiful complexity. In other words, *you are a whole recipe*! If you are focusing on one glaring thing that frustrates you about yourself, remember—that's only the tiniest fraction of who you are. There's a whole lot more that makes you, *you*! The recipe of your life includes some wonderful ingredients but also some things you may still be healing from. As we all know, this life journey contains a little bit of everything. Think about all that's mixed into your current situation: the place and time you live in, the experiences you've had, and your unique, God-created, biological makeup. And what about your relationships? Consider how some people have positively poured into your life, while others have hurt you. These are all things that have shaped who you are today. So, if you find yourself feeling discouraged about your progress in any way, remember that you're dealing with more than you probably realize, and you're doing the best you can!

Jesus loved to remind people of the depth of their lives—of the hidden things and all that was happening beneath the surface that they were unaware of. That's part of what God seems to be doing with all of us. He reminds us of everything we are and of the role that each of those things plays in our growth toward wholeness in Him.

Pursue Peace

Here's an interesting, creative exercise to try. Grab some paper and write "My Recipe" at the top. Then, think about all the things that went into making you who you are today. It may include the environment you were raised in, your family dynamic, or a few significant things that happened in your growing-up years that left their mark on your life somehow. It might be some of the achievements that have given you confidence, an illness you've struggled through, your career experience, your friendships, or your observations about your personality.

There are no rules about how to do this, so just open your mind and heart! Ask God to reveal things you may not have considered that affect your life today—both positively and negatively. The whole purpose of this exercise is to have a greater appreciation of your depth and complexity as a divinely created human being on the marvelous journey called life.

When you're having a rough day and you're tempted to focus on the parts of yourself you wish to change, remember that you are like a complex recipe. Who you are today is far more than you're able to see. And most importantly, your Maker sees it all—every facet and layer, every struggle and strength. Hear Him say to your heart: *I know exactly who you are, and I love you.*

You Can Say No

The only people who will get upset about you setting boundaries are the ones who benefited from you having none.
ANONYMOUS

And now, an important announcement about protecting yourself in this great, big world: *it's a good and healthy thing to have boundaries, and you never have to apologize for them.* Some of us had the blessing of growing up with that understanding. Our caregivers allowed (and maybe even encouraged) us to set our own limits and say no to people or situations that made us uncomfortable. They helped us learn to listen to our God-given intuition, to speak honestly, and to ask for what we needed. And whether that need was a little personal space at home or some distance from a stressful situation, we knew we could depend on our caretakers to honor our boundaries, which brought us a sense of safety and security. Others of us, however, knew little about personal space when we were young. And that's probably because those who were raising us didn't understand the importance of it either! They couldn't pass along to us what they themselves had never received as children. Many people in the generations before us were taught that showing kindness was more important than anything—even if that meant betraying themselves by doing something they knew wasn't right for them.

As adults, we may still be learning how to navigate relationships and learning to commit to loving others while protecting and providing for ourselves. All we have to do is look at Jesus's life to see a perfect example of this. He shared God's love freely, but He also honored His own needs and had no problem saying, "Guys, it's time for Me to step away for a bit and recharge."

Pursue Peace

Think of the dynamics in your relationships for a moment. First, consider your inner circle and how you interact with each person who is close to you. Are there some who tend to drain you? Are there others who may be compromising *themselves* because they're afraid to be honest with you about their needs? And what about your acquaintances—your coworkers or others who touch your life in some way? Do you feel like you're able to say *no* when you need to, or do you try to be a *yes* person at all costs? And on the flipside, do you feel like you're respectful of *their* limits and needs?

Some people will naturally feel rejected by our boundaries because they haven't had a lot of experience with them—but that's okay! All we can do is communicate our needs to others in the most loving way possible. Maybe it'll inspire others to do the same for themselves down the road. Remember: Jesus is our model for balance. He is intimately familiar with the pull between loving and caring for others and making sure our human needs are met. Anytime we feel that tension, let's ask for the reassurance and guidance that only He can give.

Healing Memories

Time doesn't heal all wounds, but Jesus does.
ANONYMOUS

The parts of you that need comfort and reassurance in your life today may feel very young and vulnerable—and that's because they've likely been with you for a long time! Think about it. When we were kids, we sometimes felt fearful and powerless. It's a great, big world we're born into, and when we're just starting out, it can feel pretty overwhelming. At some point, we all had things happen in our lives that we had no control over. Maybe we experienced some kind of sudden crisis, someone's harsh words or actions toward us, or a significant decision we had no say in that affected our future in a big way. We may have felt frightened in those moments—especially if we weren't offered the assurance we needed to know that it was all going to be okay. The adults we are today often carry those young parts of us inside, and when things happen that bring those early, painful memories to the surface, we can suddenly feel defenseless again.

One way we can help ourselves to heal is by revisiting those significant events that left their marks on our memory. We can close our eyes and envision ourselves there, but this time, we can ask Jesus to show us how He has always been with us, even before we knew His name. Whatever our hearts needed in those moments, He knew. He never left our side, even if we didn't realize it back then. And the more we can remind our younger selves of that beautiful truth, the more our grown-up selves can feel it when we face those things that threaten to rock our world—or even just our boats.

Pursue Peace

If you're up for it, why not do a little digging? Talk with your family members or lifelong friends about your childhood. See if they have anything to add to your memories. Often, just talking through your younger experiences now that you're an adult will help you to see them with a new perspective.

And when you do discover things from your early life that made their marks, consider writing a letter to your younger self about them. Fill it with the compassion, encouragement, and reassurance that you've received from God throughout the years. Tell your past self everything you needed to hear in those moments when you felt most alone and afraid. And as you observe the people around you, remember that they, too, have a younger self inside, and sometimes those things they do as adults come from old wounds that are still healing. You can choose to be the one who holds a grace-filled space for them, trusting that God is working in them just as He is working in you.

We all grow up and change, but our loving Creator remains the same "yesterday, today, and forever" (Hebrews 13:8 NLT), and that means no matter what the entire span of our lifetime holds. He is right there in it with us—in more ways than we can imagine.

Apart + Together

We live within and beyond our own skin at the same time.

BONNIE BADENOCH

It's not hard to find greater balance in our lives when we're feeling a little unsteady. A really important method is looking at the tension we're experiencing between solitude and connection. We humans are complex creatures, designed to thrive both independently and in community, but never one without the other. And because each of us tends to lean a little more in one of those two directions, it's good to remind ourselves from time to time that we truly do need both!

Some people are born with a need for more space and freedom. They're "do-it-yourselfers." They may not be big on making lots of plans with others, and if they're facing a challenge, they're more likely to try to figure it out alone than reach out for help. At the other end of the spectrum are those who are natural team players. They're the "includes." They feel a strong need to always cooperate with other people. If they're headed out for a movie, they'll probably invite you! They work well in groups, and they likely have a long list of people to call when they need to talk something through. No matter which way we lean, the life that God calls us into is a beautiful balance of both. He helps us become strong individuals—nurturing within us the courage, strength, and confidence to stand on our own and be the unique selves He created. But He *also* cultivates the relational part of us, having clearly designed us to support one another in this life. His kingdom is all about *interdependence*—a thriving community made up of one-of-a-kind souls who are learning to care for both themselves and others.

Pursue Peace

Think about the last month or so. Did you find yourself at either extreme? Were you primarily isolating yourself and trying to do life mostly on your own? Or were you mostly depending on your connections with others for support, maybe even avoiding alone time as much as possible?

Regardless of where you are in that mix, if you're looking for greater balance, it can help to reflect first on why you have your particular preferences to begin with. Interview yourself with questions like these: What do I most enjoy about being alone or being with others? What brings me anxiety about being alone or being with others? When did I first start to navigate my life this way? Has it changed much over time, and if so, why? How does living at either extreme affect my ability to experience the full life God intends for me? After thinking about your answers, surrender it all to God in prayer. Trust that He will bring you the opportunities you need in order to grow in new directions, then notice what shows up in the days to come.

Taking It All In

Bloom where you are planted.
MARY ENGELBREIT

Take a moment to look around you right now, whether you're indoors or outdoors, alone in a small room or sitting among many other people. How do your surroundings make you feel? Cozy? Peaceful? Anxious? Restless? Whether you're conscious of it or not, your environment plays a part in your experience of life at every given moment. God gave you a miraculous body with amazing senses that allow you to interact with the creation that surrounds you every day—whether that be people, places, or things. You are a sensory being, and that makes your environment vitally important because you'll always be connected to it in some way.

The truth is, we can't always choose the space we want to be in. We may be stuffed in a cubicle, surrounded by laundry, or dealing with certain people who are part of our everyday lives and we have a hard time being around. But we *can* do our best to work with what we have. During those times when we can't change locations, we can make small adjustments (both without and within) that nudge us toward a more positive experience. Becoming more aware of how our surroundings affect us is a great first step. Some of the negativity we experience in our days can have a much simpler source than we realize: it may be coming from how we feel about our atmosphere. Discovering this truth can be helpful, especially when we realize that some things are in our power to change.

Pursue Peace

Even if you spend most of your time in an environment you enjoy, there are usually little things that will bug you about it at some point. And as you've probably noticed, when you put off those little things, they can start feeling like a bigger deal than they need to! Maybe it's sorting one of those piles you've been ignoring, or finally picking out that new paint color, or washing the windows—do whatever it is that will help to bring you a greater sense of peace in your space. And if your daily environment isn't ideal, take a good look around and try to identify the things you can control. How can you add a few elements that make you smile, help you relax, or remind you to look for the blessings in your day? Maybe a plant or two if you're a nature lover, or a print of your favorite Bible verse. If there's a difficult person you encounter daily, ask God to help in that relationship. Set any boundaries you feel are necessary to avoid being drained in your interactions.

The bottom line is this: never underestimate the effect your environment has on your well-being, and always remember that the small changes you make can work together to make a big difference in the way you experience your daily life.

PAUSE FOR PRAYER

Dear Heavenly Father,

I come before You today with a heavy heart, struggling with tension and conflict in a relationship. You are the God of peace, and I need Your wisdom and grace to navigate this situation with love and understanding. When my emotions rise and my heart feels unsettled, remind me to seek You first. Help me to respond with patience, kindness, and humility instead of anger or resentment.

Lord, please soften my heart where there is hardness, and open my eyes to see others as You see them. As I seek Your peace in this situation, give me the strength to forgive as You have forgiven me and to pursue reconciliation where it is possible. Fill me with Your peace, which passes all understanding, so that I may reflect Your love, even in difficult moments.

Father, I ask that Your Spirit would guide my words and actions. Make me a peacemaker and an instrument of Your grace.

In Jesus's name, amen.

What We Think We Know

All the assumptions in the world cannot replace one single bit of truth.
ANONYMOUS

Would you describe yourself as someone who's an open book, or do you tend to be more private about your life? Many of us fall in a different place on the spectrum on any given day, depending on the circumstances and who we're with. Regardless, we can be sure of one thing: no one except our Maker knows every little thing about us, no matter how "open" we think we are! And of course, we don't know every little thing about anyone else—not even our bestie, or our spouse, or the sibling whose sentences we can pretty much finish. It's important for us to remember that when we're dealing with our opinions about others' lives and their opinions about our lives.

No one knows what it's like to live in another person's skin, but sometimes the assumptions we make about one another suggest otherwise. We may witness someone's words or actions and jump to a conclusion that isn't true. That's called misjudgment. And as we have surely noted, Jesus calls us away from judging others—regardless of whether our speculation can be confirmed. His example reminds us that no one is worthy to "throw a stone" (John 8:7 ESV) in any situation. Condemning others is simply not our job! And the more we embody this truth, the more peace we'll have inside. We will rest in the fact that He's the only One who sees everything from every angle, and it's His perspective that matters in the end.

Pursue Peace

Are we willing to honestly look at the kinds of judgments we tend to make about other people? The truth is, we may be so used to making them, we don't even realize we're doing it! Just paying attention to those thoughts when they come up is a positive step toward change. And then we can start to choose different thoughts—ones that are more grace-filled and compassionate. We can ask questions like these: Is that guy at the register grouchy because he's a terrible human, or is he going through a hard time? Is the girl who honked behind me at that red light ridiculously impatient, or is she afraid of being late? Did my friend really mean to hurt my feelings, or did her words just come out wrong?

What about choosing a simple phrase to recall when you catch yourself making assumptions? You could say to yourself, *There's more to this story than what I can see.* And when the tables are turned and someone is jumping to conclusions about you, try responding this way: *There's more to my story, and I trust that God sees the big picture!* James 2:13 (NIV) reminds us of the oft-forgotten truth that "mercy triumphs over judgment." Be someone who stands on that truth in your life and watch how it inspires others to do the same.

How to Be Still

God speaks in the silence of the heart. Listening is the beginning of prayer.

MOTHER TERESA

Be still, and know that I am God" (Psalm 46:10 NIV) is a beloved and well-known verse for good reason. It calms us and reminds us that God is never asking us to perform for Him or try to be more than we are. This simple truth can set the tone for everything else in our lives. But it's easy to forget that the *knowing* part of that verse comes only *after* the *being still* part. First, He invites us to enter stillness. Only then can we "know" as we become deeply aware of His comforting presence.

If you've ever tried practicing stillness—whether to pray and hear from God or to reflect on His Word—you may have learned that it can be really tough to stop and pause; it's hard for many of us to sit with ourselves and our thoughts for very long. Once we turn off the screens and other distractions around us and still our bodies, we become keenly aware of how often our minds overthink and how our thought cycles and obsessions function like a hamster on a wheel. Many of us can only take a few minutes of that total stillness and silence before we reach for something to distract us. Learning to be present in the moment is an exercise for the spirit, just as a workout is for the physical body. We may have to ease into it to build those inner muscles, but the longer we can settle into that simple awareness, the more of God's wonderful peace we can feel.

Pursue Peace

Consider setting aside a few minutes today to quietly sit and just *be* in God's presence. See what happens. If your mind starts to chatter—which tends to happen for most of us—try watching whatever appears as an observer might. Imagine a stream or a breeze or whatever comes to mind as something that could move those thoughts along and out of your sight. Just watch them flow away and trust that anything needing attention will be resolved in God's time. Right now, your intention is to let everything else go in order to make space for your simple awareness of Him.

As your mind naturally wanders, don't judge it or overly exert yourself to rein it in. Just take a deep breath and simply come back to where you're sitting. Again and again. Sense God's quiet presence with you. Understand that He is delighting in your company, just as you delight in His. You may even feel it in your heart to smile and soak in the warmth of His loving gaze. For some people, having a phrase or short verse to say helps them focus. These can be very simple thoughts, like, *Thank You, Jesus*, which lifts our hearts in gratitude, or, *God's peace is with me*, which reminds us of the very real connection we share with Him.

Always Worthy

Your worth and people's approval are two different things.
Learn to separate the two.
BRITTNEY MOSES

One way we can tell just how grounded we are in who God created us to be is by observing what happens when others claim to be disappointed by us. Whether it's an acquaintance, a coworker, or someone in our inner circle, it can be really painful when they look at us with a face that says, "You dropped the ball." But guess what? As hard as we try, we will all fall short sometimes. Before we allow ourselves to fall into the rabbit hole of thinking, *I'm not good enough*, or, *I'll never get it right*, it's important to consider the details of whatever disappointing thing just happened. Sure, it may simply be that we messed something up unintentionally—we forgot an important event, didn't finish something on time, or weren't available when someone needed us. These things happen because we are human beings managing complex lives in a busy world.

Sometimes, though, it isn't about us at all. Sometimes others are disappointed in us because of their unrealistic expectations. We can find great comfort in remembering this. Even if someone points a finger at us, it's not a burden we need to bear. They may have set the bar impossibly high and expected us to deliver beyond our ability. Or maybe they have a hard time admitting that *they're* the ones who missed the mark, so they try to make it about someone else. Our Creator is the only One who can truly understand our motives. He calls us to draw close in times like these so He can speak the truth to our hearts and offer the assurance and guidance that only He can give.

Pursue Peace

If we want to live with less fear about "messing up" in our lives, it all starts with laying a solid foundation of sacred self-worth—standing on the truth of who God says we are. What about finding a few "love notes" that God has written to us in His Word and keeping them close? After you've selected some verses that describe God's love for you, consider making a list of the things that *you* love about yourself. Ask yourself things like, "What natural gifts has God given me, and how am I using them? What are some unique things about myself that make me smile? How do I bring joy to those around me daily?"

The next time you find yourself in a disappointing situation, stop for a moment and ask yourself, "What's really going on?" If there are amends to be made, ask God for the courage and grace to make them and move on, trusting that He sees your heart and never withdraws an ounce of His love, no matter how anyone else feels about you. In the end, no matter what happens, or how, or with whom . . . you can trust that God sees your intentions. He is always working to bring about the greatest good for you and everyone involved because we all have infinite worth in His eyes.

Silver Linings

If you don't like something, change it.
If you can't change it, change your attitude.
MAYA ANGELOU

God always gives us a choice when we feel disappointment or discouragement creeping in: we can resent the situation that brought it about and allow it to drag us down, or we can accept what is and let it be a stepping-stone toward something greater. We've all had some disheartening times—whether it be work stresses, raising children, financial uncertainty, or even the opportunities we once had that are no longer available. On one hand, we may experience some of these changes as positive ones. Maybe we needed a little wake-up call to do things differently in life. But on the other hand, we may feel like the life we're living now isn't how we wanted it to be at all. We had plans that were derailed and ideas that never became realities. It's natural to feel the deep disappointment of unfulfilled dreams. The pull toward *what might have been* can be really strong when we haven't yet found peace with *what is.*

To be clear, accepting where we are today doesn't mean settling or giving up. It doesn't mean not hoping for more or not pursuing the dreams we know God has hidden within us. Acceptance is just that moment of looking around and saying from our hearts, "This is my life right now, and I'm trusting that God knows exactly what's happening." It's where we find our solid footing in reality before we take that first step on the next leg of the journey. It's where we meet Him in the "now" of our lives and say, "I'm okay with my present circumstances, and I'm trusting You to guide me into what's next."

Pursue Peace

Centuries after Paul reminded us to "give thanks in all circumstances" (I Thessalonians 5:18 NIV), gratitude is still recognized as one of the main pillars of a happy life. And those times when we find ourselves feeling frustrated and ungrateful are the times that can transform us beautifully. The low points in our lives can be like red flags reminding us that we need to shift our focus from our lack to our abundance.

Set aside a few minutes in your day to make a list of the things that you wish were different in your life right now. It might be a commute to work, a spirit-squashing neighbor who loves to rain on your parade, a health issue, or a financial burden. Just get it all out so you can tell yourself the truth about it. Talk to God about your frustrations. Be honest about the changes you're hoping for, but also ask for the grace to accept what *is*—just as it is—today.

Then, make one more list of things you are grateful for in the life you're living right here, right now. That will be your "silver linings" list. If you make it a regular practice to look for blessings every day, you'll be surprised at how much brighter the world gets—not because your circumstances change, but because your perspective does.

Inside Out

Integrity gives you real freedom because you have nothing to fear, since you have nothing to hide.

ZIG ZIGLAR

Here's an important connection you may have noticed in your life: the more integrity you choose to live with, the more peace you get to enjoy. Consider this definition of *integrity*: "The state of being whole and undivided." That means it's more than just a moral standard—more than our actions aligning with our words. It's also living in a way that our inside matches our outside. The words we speak *reveal* the truth we carry within; they don't *hide* it. When we open our mouths, are we doing so with honesty, or are we telling people what they want to hear? Are we flattering with our tongues but resenting with our hearts?

Anytime we lean toward "faking it" in any way, we take on the burden of managing a façade, and that can drain our sense of peace in a big way. When we find ourselves praying for a calmer spirit in our daily lives, we need to remember that a calm spirit is the fruit of an integrated life. We weren't designed to live with division within, and when we do, it can cause a lot of stress and anxiety. We were created to thrive as whole beings like Jesus did, and that means learning more and more to "speak the truth in love" (Ephesians 4:15 NLT). The more our lives flow with integrity, the less friction we'll experience between the true and the false, and the less energy we'll spend trying to fill the gap between who we really are on the inside and who we're pretending to be on the outside. Our relationships will become more authentic because there's nothing left to hide.

Pursue Peace

You've probably heard the saying, "If you can't say anything nice, don't say anything at all." But if you replace the word *nice* with *truthful* and read it again, that phrase really gets to the heart of the matter. It's not about saying *nice* things in order to spare someone's feelings; it's about sharing honest words (even if it takes courage to speak them) in order to help bring about God's highest good for everyone.

Try asking yourself these questions: How often do I speak just to fill the silence? How often do I say what I think other people want to hear instead of being honest about my feelings? Am I able to relax and enjoy most conversations with others, or do I have a sense of anxiety about expressing myself? When I think of my most significant relationships, how clear and direct is the communication?

Only you know how truthfully you're showing up in the world, but one thing is certain: you're a work in progress. We all are! Even if today you feel more limited in your self-expression, God is always inviting you to take steps toward greater integrity. He knows that the more authentically you show up in your life, the greater sense of peace and freedom you will enjoy.

PAUSE FOR PRAYER

Dear Lord Jesus,

Thank You for being my constant Source of peace, even in the small frustrations and challenges of daily life on this earth. Sometimes I let worry, impatience, and stress steal my joy over things that don't truly matter. But You call me to rest in You, to trust that You are present in every moment, big or small.

Lord, when unexpected inconveniences arise, help me to respond with grace rather than frustration. When my plans don't go as I hoped, remind me that Your plans are always better. When I feel overwhelmed by responsibilities, give me the strength to take just one step at a time, knowing that You walk beside me.

Continue to fill my heart with Your peace, Lord. Let it flow through my words, my actions, and my thoughts. Help me to view the events of my life—every day of it—through the lens of Your love, embracing each moment with gratitude and trust.

In Your precious name I pray.

Amen.

Our Only Constant

In any given moment, we have two options:
to step forward into growth or step back into safety.
ABRAHAM MASLOW

Have you ever watched kids on a merry-go-round or other amusement park rides? The moment things start moving, everyone reaches for something to hold on to. We humans (big and small) have that tendency—a natural instinct to steady ourselves when we're thrown off balance unexpectedly. This is what happens when we face change or uncertainty in our lives. We often look for something or someone to hold on to—to calm and reassure us, and to remind us that we are safe, even if things feel a bit chaotic at the moment. As we all know, this will likely happen more than once on this unpredictable path we call "life." Because, given enough time, everything changes: our relationships, our circumstances, our perspectives, even our spiritual journeys.

It's been said that the only constant in life is change, but if we really think about it, we know that's not true. Because there's another, even more *constant*, constant! And it's not a thing; it's our God. The One "who is, and who was, and who is to come" (Revelation 1:8 NIV) is the firm foundation in our lives that we can always return to when we need to find sure footing again. Trusting God's love and sovereignty over every other thing that comes our way can completely transform our experience of life's transitions. We can embrace change and focus more and more on what our heavenly Father is doing through it all—how He's guiding us, helping us grow, protecting us, and offering us His peace along the way.

Pursue Peace

We can witness the beauty of transformation in nature. When you find yourself feeling a sense of doubt or uncertainty about changes happening in your life, try spending a little time outdoors. Watch how all of creation ebbs and flows and how things that fall to the ground take root and grow again in another form. Just by looking at a seed or a cocoon, it's impossible to guess what magnificent growth and metamorphosis is taking place within. Perhaps that's one reason why many of us are drawn to the great outdoors—creation is one way God reveals truths to us about how all of life works, including our own!

If you're not an outdoorsy sort of person, you can take your observations indoors. There's plenty of creation in there, too, including the people who surround you! Watch how their relationships play out and how every day is a new challenge to meet or celebration to experience together. When you're sitting at an airport, a party, or a family get-together, think about all the dynamics that go into those human connections. Showing up for our lives (and for each other) in a constantly changing world is no small thing. We all walk through times of vulnerability, and we all need reminders that through it all, we can count on the loving, sustaining presence of our Maker.

Forgiving You

Lighten up on yourself. No one is perfect. Gently accept your humanness.

DEBORAH DAY

The Bible reminds us more than a few times about the importance of forgiveness—how it frees the person we've chosen to forgive but also frees us from holding a grudge we're not meant to carry; how we imitate God when we take that first step toward reconciliation (no matter how much we want to run in the other direction sometimes); and even how we may be tired of forgiving someone repeatedly, but as Jesus says to Peter in Matthew 18:22 (NLT), we're called to forgive not "seven times . . . but seventy times seven." (In other words, a *whole bunch of times!*)

Here's something to remember when you think about giving grace like that: There's someone you may be forgetting who needs your forgiveness more often than you realize. It's someone who can feel pretty discouraged at times, who is well aware that they aren't perfect but who needs unconditional love and compassion just like everybody else. And guess what? That someone is *you.*

Forgiving ourselves can be tricky because often the resentment we carry within us is hidden, and we're not aware of how it's affecting us. It's not played out through an outward relationship with another person whom we feel wronged us. It's the *internal* struggle we feel as the result of something we wish we hadn't done. Some of us have needed to experience reconciliation within for a long time. Because here's the thing: *other* people have forgiven us, we know God *always* forgives us, but if we're still holding something against *ourselves*, it can be hard to fully receive God's grace.

Pursue Peace

We hear plenty about the importance of forgiving others, and rightly so. In a culture where many may be quick to condemn and slow to offer compassion, we can shine the light of Christ brightly by giving grace in tough situations. But let us always remember that it has to start within ourselves. So, how about you and your heart? Is there anything unresolved that could use some tender loving care? Read the following verses and think about them in the context of self-forgiveness:

- *"Hatred stirs up strife, but love covers all offenses"* (Proverbs 10:12 NASB).
- *"Therefore there is now no condemnation at all for those who are in Christ Jesus"* (Romans 8:1 NASB).
- *"Be kind and compassionate to one another, forgiving each other, just as in Christ God forgave you"* (Ephesians 4:32 NIV).
- *"As far as the east is from the west, so far has He removed our transgressions from us"* (Psalm 103:12 NIV).

Your heavenly Father is surely willing and always able to release you from whatever you might be holding against yourself. Remember, the person looking back at you in the mirror is infinitely precious to Him, and He delights in helping you let go of anything that holds you back from living more freely in His love.

Family Matters

Rejoice with your family in the beautiful land of life!

ALBERT EINSTEIN

Can we talk about family for a moment? How's it going with yours? The people we call "family" often have a significant impact on the quality of our lives, and it's good to reflect now and then on the strength and health of those specific relationships. At some point in your life, you probably discovered that there are no "normal" families. Of course, some of us came from what is considered a stable family, and others came from more turbulent backgrounds. Regardless of the environment we grew up in, it is easy to look at the other side of things and make assumptions. For example, it's easy to assume that nice families never have problems or that troubled families produce troubled kids. But the truth is that every small group of people sharing four walls and a roof is going to have lots of different things to work through. Plus, those little groups are connected to other relatives who bring something to the mix. The bottom line is this: *families can be complicated!*

How about you? What kind of life did you have growing up? If you came from a warm and loving home, what a gift! Hopefully you're able to pass that gift along to your own children or to others who didn't have the blessing of a stable family life. Or maybe you didn't grow up with a sense of safety and belonging. Maybe you struggle with it even today. If that's the case, please know that your heavenly Father desires to provide those loving connections for you. You are part of His eternal family, after all, and you can sense His wonderful assurance throughout your life in many ways.

Pursue Peace

Think about the people you consider to be your family. Whether they live in your home or are scattered around the globe, whether you have the same blood, share a deep friendship, or are brothers and sisters in Christ, those connections are gifts from God, and His Word reminds us of the importance of nurturing them. It's good to remember that when we've asked Him to provide for our needs in the past, these connections have often been answers to those prayers.

Try making a list of the most special people in your life, and beside each name write one thing you might do to connect with them more intentionally. It could be something as simple as a nightly hug or a weekly text—whatever might communicate how precious they are to you. The positive effect those loving gestures can have on our relationships is greater than we may realize.

And what about your end of things? Do you feel loved and nurtured by those you share your life with? Are there needs *you* have that you haven't expressed? Ask God to show you how you can more fully experience the lifelong, soul-deep relationships He provides. Lean into Him when you find yourself struggling, for He is always there with reassurance, guidance, and grace, offering you a place in His heart to call home.

To Tell You the Truth

Honesty is more than not lying. It is truth telling,
truth speaking, truth living, and truth loving.
JAMES E. FAUST

Here's something important to consider when we're going through tough times: God often provides comfort and encouragement through the people around us, but they won't know to comfort and encourage us if they don't realize how much we need it. And that requires us to be honest about how we feel, especially on our hard days.

Think about it. When you say, "How are you?" to other people, do you notice how often they give an automatic "I'm fine" response? What about you? When someone asks you about yourself, do you have an automatic response prepared? Do you ever wish you could just say how you really feel on rough days? And if you *did*, do you think it might get awkward? The truth is, it probably would—at least for a moment or two. And that's because giving a real, from-the-heart answer requires more than small talk, and a lot of us would rather keep it on the surface. Those autopilot conversations feel comfortable and safe, and most of us are so used to them, we don't even think about what we are saying! But we always have an opportunity during those encounters to offer a little more of ourselves. In fact, doing so can not only open the door for others to encourage us but also inspire them to be honest about their own feelings when they are the ones struggling. And as we all know, everybody struggles sometimes.

Pursue Peace

We often encounter people who have something they need to express, but they hold it in instead. They may feel that no one has the time to listen, or even if others did listen, they might not understand. You might know what that feels like too. Carrying a burden alone creates a sense of heaviness and loneliness in our lives that we weren't intended to bear.

Start paying close attention to the automatic responses people give in conversations. Look into their eyes. Get a sense of their sincerity. Next time someone answers "fine" to your "How are you?" and you can clearly see that they're *not* fine, consider taking a moment to press in and say, "Are you *sure*?" See if they might want to share more. It doesn't have to turn into an hour-long conversation. It may just be a few moments of much-needed connection, an offer of a hug, or even a promise to pray for them. It's amazing the difference a small gesture can make. And when the tables are turned, let's try to keep ourselves open to the support that others offer us too. The more openly and honestly we live, the more space we make for the comfort and encouragement God sends our way through those who touch our lives.

The Send-Off

For Jesus doesn't change—yesterday, today, tomorrow,
He's always totally Himself.

HEBREWS 13:8 THE MESSAGE

"I am Alpha and Omega, the beginning and the end, the first and the last" (Revelation 22:13 KJV). What could comfort us more than these words of Jesus, which are filled with all the reassurance we will ever need? His infinite love bookends this life we're living. *Everything* begins and ends in Him—our very being, our first breath, and our first real steps of faith—every day of our lives. He is the beginning—the source behind the sunrise, the catalyst for our growth, healing, and wholeness as cherished children of God.

And He is our destination. We are always headed toward His open arms and grace-filled heart. Everything that happens on this journey of life leads us home to Him. We may feel uncertainty along the way. We may feel beat down by discouragement, confused by doubt, and hindered by fear, but those things will never have the last word. His Word is the last word. The promises we stand on are not wishes or temporary fixes or great ideas for how to get through life a little easier. They are what our faith is made of—"the substance of things hoped for, the evidence of things not seen" (Hebrews 11:1 KJV). The truth of God is the most substantial, reliable, and unchanging force in the universe, and it is available to us daily in His presence, His creation, and His Word. Hold on to that truth tightly when you feel alone or afraid or misunderstood. When you need comfort, know how closely you are being held and guided by the One who loves you more than you could possibly imagine.

Pursue Peace

Our Creator provides many ways for us to grow in faith, love, and freedom throughout our lives, but we always have the choice how to respond. We can choose to remain stuck in the familiar patterns we may have lived with for a long time, or we can open ourselves up to more life-giving ways of being in the world. We can choose to see our challenges as negative experiences to avoid at all costs, or we can embrace whatever comes and allow Him to use our hardships for our healing—just as He intends.

We know a calmer spirit doesn't develop in a single, miraculous moment. It's often the result of walking through trials—learning to weather life's storms hand in hand with the One who allows them. We must keep our eyes on Jesus, not the trials we face. His hand is forever outstretched to steady and reassure us. He's not calling us to take a detour or to find a way of escape from the hard things. He's leading us right through it all. He's asking us to turn our eyes toward Him and put our trust in Him every single day. And as a result, we will experience the soul-soothing peace and deep joy that can only come from surrendering our lives to the God who knows and loves us best.

Comfort Promises & Prayers by DaySpring™

No matter what you are facing today, you can rest in knowing the Creator of the universe loves you. He loves you deeply and perfectly with absolutely no conditions. And He's made hundreds of promises to you!

Below you'll find the 100 most referenced verses we turn to again and again for encouragement, joy, and strength.

For your convenience, we've provided a quick reference guide—a unique tool that makes it easy for you to find just the right comfort promises for your immediate need.

When you are AFRAID . . .

He will not allow your foot to slip; He who keeps you will not slumber.
PSALM 121:3 NASB

"Do not fear; I will help you."
ISAIAH 41:13 NIV

Draw near to God, and He will draw near to you.
JAMES 4:8 CSB

When you are ANXIOUS . . .

"If you follow Me, you won't have to walk in darkness, because you will have the light that leads to life."
JOHN 8:12 NLT

Don't fret or worry. Instead of worrying, pray.
PHILIPPIANS 4:6 THE MESSAGE

He never changes or casts a shifting shadow.
JAMES 1:17 NLT

When you need ASSURANCE . . .

He is the faithful God, keeping His covenant of love to a thousand generations.
DEUTERONOMY 7:9 NIV

"You're blessed when you're at the end of your rope. With less of you there is more of God."
MATTHEW 5:3 THE MESSAGE

He chose us . . . that we would be holy and blameless before Him.
EPHESIANS 1:4 NASB

You are saved by grace through faith . . . it is God's gift.
EPHESIANS 2:8 CSB

He cares about you.
I PETER 5:7 NLT

His divine power has given us everything required for life.
II PETER 1:3 CSB

When you need COMFORT . . .

The Lord is near the brokenhearted; He saves those crushed in spirit.
PSALM 34:18 CSB

Take delight in the Lord, and He will give you your heart's desires.
PSALM 37:4 CSB

"My faithful love for you will remain. My covenant of blessing will never be broken."
ISAIAH 54:10 NLT

"I have it all planned out—plans to take care of you, not abandon you, plans to give you the future you hope for."
JEREMIAH 29:11 THE MESSAGE

He will rejoice over you with gladness. . . . He will delight in you with singing.
ZEPHANIAH 3:17 CSB

"Blessed are those who mourn, for they shall be comforted."
MATTHEW 5:4 ESV

He comforts us in all our troubles so that we can comfort others.
II CORINTHIANS 1:4 NLT

God chose you to be the holy people He loves.
COLOSSIANS 3:12 NLT

When you need COURAGE . . .

You, Lord, are a shield around me, my glory, and the One who lifts up my head.
PSALM 3:3 CSB

I can do everything through Christ, who gives me strength.
PHILIPPIANS 4:13 NLT

He hears their cry for help and saves them.
PSALM 145:19 CSB

"I will strengthen you, I will help you, I will uphold you with my righteous right hand."
ISAIAH 41:10 ESV

This is what the LORD says, he who made the earth, the LORD who formed it and established it—the LORD is His name: "Call to Me and I will answer you and tell you great and unsearchable things you do not know."
JEREMIAH 33:2–3 NIV

The LORD is good to those who wait for Him, to the person who seeks Him.
LAMENTATIONS 3:25 NASB

"I will send you the Advocate—the Spirit of truth. He will come to you from the Father and will testify all about Me."
JOHN 15:26 NLT

He hears us.
I JOHN 5:14 NASB

When you need HOPE . . .

The LORD will fight for you while you keep silent.
EXODUS 14:14 NASB

"Be strong; don't give up, for your work has a reward."
II CHRONICLES 15:7 CSB

The LORD grants favor and honor; He does not withhold the good from those who live with integrity.
PSALM 84:11 CSB

He has made everything beautiful in its time.
ECCLESIASTES 3:11 NIV

His mercies never end. They are new every morning.
LAMENTATIONS 3:22–23 CSB

"I am the living bread . . . Whoever eats this bread will live forever."
JOHN 6:51 NIV

"Anyone who believes in Me will live, even after dying."
JOHN 11:25 NLT

We have this hope as an anchor for the soul, firm and secure.
HEBREWS 6:19 NIV

When you need JOY . . .

Do not grieve, for the joy of the Lord is your strength.
NEHEMIAH 8:10 NIV

You will fill me with joy in Your presence.
PSALM 16:11 NIV

You turned my lament into dancing.
PSALM 30:11 CSB

"Give, and it will be given to you."
LUKE 6:38 NIV

When you are LONELY . . .

He will be with you; He will not leave you or abandon you.
DEUTERONOMY 31:8 CSB

"The Lord your God is with you wherever you go."
JOSHUA 1:9 CSB

He Himself has said, "I will never leave you or abandon you."
HEBREWS 13:5 CSB

When you are feeling OVERWHELMED . . .

Nothing will be impossible with God.
LUKE 1:37 ESV

The God of all grace . . . will himself restore, confirm, strengthen, and establish you.
I PETER 5:10 ESV

When you need PEACE . . .

The Lord gives His people strength; the Lord blesses His people with peace.
PSALM 29:11 CSB

"Peace I leave with you. My peace I give to you."
JOHN 14:27 CSB

His peace will guard your hearts and minds as you live in Christ Jesus.
PHILIPPIANS 4:7 NLT

When you need PROTECTION . . .

You are a hiding place for me; you preserve me from trouble.
PSALM 32:7 ESV

All humanity finds shelter in the shadow of Your wings.
PSALM 36:7 NLT

God has not given us a spirit of fear, but one of power, love, and sound judgment.
II TIMOTHY 1:7 CSB

Humble yourselves
before the Lord, and
He will lift you up.
JAMES 4:10 NIV

When you need ENCOURAGEMENT . . .

His faithful love
endures forever.
PSALM 100:5 CSB

"I will be your God
throughout your
lifetime—until your hair
is white with age."
ISAIAH 46:4 NLT

"I will give you a new
heart and put a new
spirit within you."
EZEKIEL 36:26 CSB

I am convinced that neither
death nor life, neither angels
nor demons, neither the
present nor the future, nor
any powers, neither height
nor depth, nor anything
else in all creation, will be
able to separate us from
the love of God that is in
Christ Jesus our Lord.
ROMANS 8:38–39 NIV

He will not let you be
tempted beyond your ability.
I CORINTHIANS 10:13 ESV

He has created us anew
in Christ Jesus, so we
can do the good things
He planned for us.
EPHESIANS 2:10 NLT

When you need FORGIVENESS . . .

"I will forgive their sin
and will heal their land."
II CHRONICLES 7:14 NIV

"Though your sins are
scarlet, they will be
as white as snow."
ISAIAH 1:18 CSB

By giving Himself
completely at the Cross,
actually dying for you,
Christ brought you over to
God's side and put your
lives together, whole and
holy in His presence.
COLOSSIANS 1:22 THE MESSAGE

He . . . will forgive us
our sins and purify us.
I JOHN 1:9 NIV

God, who . . . will bring
you with great joy into
His glorious presence
without a single fault.
JUDE 1:24 NLT

When you need GUIDANCE . . .

He will make your paths straight.
PROVERBS 3:6 CSB

The Lord will continually guide you.
ISAIAH 58:11 NASB

"When the Spirit of truth comes, He will guide you into all truth."
JOHN 16:13 NLT

When you need HEALING . . .

He heals the brokenhearted and binds up their wounds.
PSALM 147:3 ESV

By His wounds we are healed.
ISAIAH 53:5 NIV

"I will give you back your health and heal your wounds."
JEREMIAH 30:17 NLT

When you need HELP . . .

"I will send you rain in its season, and the ground will yield its crops and the trees their fruit."
LEVITICUS 26:4 NIV

Day after day He bears our burdens.
PSALM 68:19 CSB

He will give His angels orders . . . to protect you in all your ways.
PSALM 91:11 CSB

The Lord will guard your going out and your coming in from this time forth and forever.
PSALM 121:8 NASB

He is a shield to those who take refuge in Him.
PROVERBS 30:5 CSB

A stronghold for the poor . . . a refuge from storms and a shade from heat.
ISAIAH 25:4 CSB

"No weapon turned against you will succeed."
ISAIAH 54:17 NLT

He will strengthen you and protect you.
II THESSALONIANS 3:3 NIV

When you need REST and RENEWAL . . .

The LORD is my shepherd, I lack nothing. He makes me lie down in green pastures, He leads me beside quiet waters.
PSALM 23:1–2 NIV

He renews my life; He leads me along the right paths for His name's sake.
PSALM 23:3 CSB

He satisfies you with good things; your youth is renewed like the eagle.
PSALM 103:5 CSB

Those who wait for the LORD will gain new strength; they will mount up with wings like eagles, they will run and not get tired, they will walk and not become weary.
ISAIAH 40:31 NASB

"Come to me, all who labor and are heavy laden, and I will give you rest."
MATTHEW 11:28 ESV

"The Son of Man came to find and restore the lost."
LUKE 19:10 THE MESSAGE

Jesus answered, "Everyone who drinks this water will be thirsty again, but whoever drinks the water I give them will never thirst. Indeed, the water I give them will become in them a spring of water welling up to eternal life."
JOHN 4:13–14 NIV

Our inner person is being renewed day by day.
II CORINTHIANS 4:16 CSB

If anyone is in Christ, he is a new creation.
II CORINTHIANS 5:17 CSB

When you need STRENGTH . . .

He gives power to the weak and strength to the powerless.
ISAIAH 40:29 NLT

The Spirit helps us in our weakness.
ROMANS 8:26 ESV

He will keep you strong to the end so that you will be free from all blame on the day when our Lord Jesus Christ returns.
I CORINTHIANS 1:8 NLT

When you are SUFFERING . . .

He will sustain you; He will never allow the righteous to be shaken.
PSALM 55:22 NASB

As a father has compassion on his children, so the Lord has compassion on those who fear Him; for He knows how we are formed, He remembers that we are dust.
PSALM 103:13–14 NIV

"I will be with you . . . . When you walk through the fire, you will not be scorched."
ISAIAH 43:2 CSB

"I will be your God throughout your lifetime—until your hair is white with age."
ISAIAH 46:4 NLT

The Lord is good, a stronghold in the day of trouble.
NAHUM 1:7 ESV

"Remain in Me, and I will remain in you."
JOHN 15:4 NLT

When you need WISDOM . . .

"Keep on asking, and you will receive what you ask for. Keep on seeking, and you will find. Keep on knocking, and the door will be opened to you."
MATTHEW 7:7 NLT

It is because of Him that you are in Christ Jesus, who has become for us wisdom from God—that is, our righteousness, holiness and redemption.
I CORINTHIANS 1:30 NIV

Now if any of you lacks wisdom, he should ask God . . . and it will be given to him.
JAMES 1:5 CSB

When you are WORRIED . . .

"Your Father knows exactly what you need even before you ask Him!"
MATTHEW 6:8 NLT

God will meet all your needs.
PHILIPPIANS 4:19 NIV

Dear Friend,

This book was prayerfully crafted with you, the reader, in mind. Every word, every sentence, every page was thoughtfully written, designed, and packaged to encourage you—right where you are this very moment. At DaySpring, our vision is to see every person experience the life-changing message of God's love. So, as we worked through rough drafts, design changes, edits, and details, we prayed for you to deeply experience His unfailing love, indescribable peace, and pure joy. It is our sincere hope that through these Truth-filled pages your heart will be blessed, knowing that God cares about you—your desires and disappointments, your challenges and dreams.

He knows. He cares. He loves you unconditionally.

BLESSINGS!
THE DAYSPRING BOOK TEAM